I Confess

A Memoir of the Siege of Tobruk

BIG SKY PUBLISHING
www.bigskypublishing.com.au

Major General John Joseph Murray, DSO & Bar, MC, VD 2011

Big Sky Publishing Pty Ltd
PO Box 303, Newport, NSW 2106, Australia
Phone: (61 2) 9918 2168
Fax: (61 2) 9918 2396
Email: info@bigskypublishing.com.au
Web: www.bigskypublishing.com.au

Cover design and typesetting: Think Productions

National Library of Australia Cataloguing-in-Publication entry
Author: Murray, John Joseph, 1892-1951.
Title: I confess : a memoir of the siege of Tobruk / Major General John Joseph Murray, DSO & Bar, MC, VD.
ISBN: 9780987057488 (pbk.)
Notes: Includes index.
Subjects: Australia. Army. Division, 9th.
Australia. Army. Australian Imperial Force, 2nd (1939-1946)
Tobruk, Battles of, 1941-1942.
World War, 1939-1945--Campaigns--Africa, North.
World War, 1939-1945--Participation, Australian.
World War, 1939-1945--Regimental histories--Australia.
Dewey Number: 940.5423
Printed in China through Bookbuilders

I Confess

A Memoir of the Siege of Tobruk

BIG SKY PUBLISHING
www.bigskypublishing.com.au

Major General John Joseph Murray, DSO & Bar, MC, VD 2011

THE AUSTRALIAN ARMY HISTORY COLLECTION

PROTECTING ARMY HERITAGE
PROMOTING ARMY HISTORY

Dedicated to my wife Madeline who, had she known this book was being written, would have done all in her power to prevent its publication.

My Daily Prayer

Oh Lord, I pray that I might have the gift to understand the men with whom I have to deal, their frailties, their doubts, their fears, and that together we might find the strength to be true to our ideals.

J.J. Murray

Editorial Note

I Confess is a memoir written by my grandfather, Major General John Joseph Murray, DSO & Bar, MC, VD, in April 1945 to record his experiences as Commander of the 20th Brigade, 9th Division, during the siege of Tobruk. The original manuscript was typed in upper case on an Army typewriter while the memories were still fresh in his mind. This version has been produced from an OCR scan of a later typed version that has been closely corrected to the original manuscript. The changes that John made to the typed manuscript by hand have been incorporated. It has been copy edited for publication ensuring that the distinctive voice of the author colours this version as it did the original. Thus it remains faithful to the original manuscript, including only the following changes:

1. The text has been adjusted to a mixture of upper and lower case as appropriate. Some issues of capitalisation of military terms may remain but have been accommodated to current standards.

2. Spelling of place names has been adjusted to current practice. For instance, John varied his spelling of Tobruk, using 'Tobruc' or 'Tobruch' interchangeably. 'Tobruk' has been established in this version.

3. Spelling errors and punctuation have been corrected.

4. Two poems noted for inclusion in the manuscript and written by Hughie Paterson, son of A. B. 'Banjo' Paterson and John Joseph's driver at Tobruk, have been incorporated into the text.

David Coombes has graciously contributed a Foreword, which outlines John Joseph Murray's military service with particular attention to the siege of Tobruk. An Epilogue also expands the context of John's life and family. The memoir is further supplemented by Appendices containing original documents from the Mistral Avenue File, a file of papers and photographs kept by John after the Second World War that were clearly significant to him.

I am grateful to Anna Crookston, Mary Roddy and Leigh Gemmell and members of the Army History Unit for work on text and photos. The Australian War Memorial has assisted with images from the Mistral Avenue File and with other photographic materials. The Bathurst RSL Sub-Branch and its Museum Curator, Denis Chamberlain, have permitted images from the album, 'March: Ingleburn – Bathurst, August 1940', to be used in the text.

I am also grateful to the Army History Unit for undertaking publication of the memoir and to the publisher, Denny Neave, and the staff of Big Sky Publishing for the efficient and effective way in which they have produced the book.

Andrew Murray
7 April 2011

Author's Preface

As a man approaches his wiser years, and especially if he be in the Army, he finds himself surrounded by his friends, then the conversation often turns back to those events, often very minute in themselves, which stand out vividly. The favourite emotion of all is laughter, and in all kinds of situations, serious though some may be, there is usually some humour close by, if only one can see it.

I have the honour to number among my personal friends men who range from the private soldier to the highest ranking officers. From all of these I have not only accumulated a goodly amount of knowledge — or should I say human understanding — but I have also shared in their humour, privations, tragedies and that compassionate feeling which finds all men together when separated from those they love most dearly.

But when I get together with my friends we do not discuss the sadness, the hardships, but rather do we recall the humour of situations, practical jokes that we played or had played on us, and the highly ludicrous positions in which we have sometimes innocently found ourselves.

I have enjoyed life, which to me has been a serious, at times almost grim struggle. There has been quite a lot of tragedy in it — but I have lived fully every moment. I am writing this book for one reason only and that is to attempt to tell a tale of a soldier's life — not from a war historian's point of view, but rather from the standpoint of a raconteur of human feelings. I do not wish to delude any reader at the outset in that it might be thought that, as this book is written by a soldier, it is written about the war. Far more able pens have written on strategy, tactical situations and the chronological data that are especially applicable to war books. The war only came into this book because I am using it as a foundation on which to write of my friends and acquaintances and other people whom I have met under certain conditions — mainly those that contain a human interest.

I believe in the economists' theory of a division of labour. I have written this book; it is up to you to read it. In its compilation I have been assisted and helped in various ways by many kindly people without whose guidance I would have been at a considerable disadvantage.

I can only hope that the sensitivities of any person mentioned have not been offended in any way. I regard them all as my friends and, should any exception be taken, they have my humblest apologies. I trust that you take the same pleasure from reading it as I have had in writing it — here's happy reading to you.

Studio Portrait of Major General John Joseph Murray (NX365). Post WW2. John Murray collection.

Foreword

Major General John Joseph Murray is a little known but important figure in Australian military history. Not only did he serve his country with distinction in two world wars, Murray gave of his time between the wars helping organise and train recruits in the Australian Citizen Military Forces.

When war was declared in August 1914, he immediately volunteered for service in the First AIF. Murray then was 22 years of age. By March 1916 he had been promoted to captain – commanding B Coy attached to 53rd Battalion, 14th Brigade (5th Australian Division).

Murray's first taste of combat was on that dreadful day at Fromelles – 19 July 1916 when, during one night, 5,533 Australian soldiers were either killed, wounded or captured. Murray was awarded the Military Cross for his deeds. Yet some controversy remains about the way he conducted himself during the battle. When interviewed, after the war, Private J.A. Giles recalled 'that it was really through this officer [Murray] that the white flag was flown by our fellows.' Certainly, the battalion's second-in-command, Major R.O. Cowey, was said to be so 'ferocious' how Murray wanted to surrender himself and his men to the enemy that, in Cowey's words, 'I flourished my revolver at him and ... intend[ed] to have him arrested at the time in case he caused disaffection in the firing line: but thought that perhaps he'd had his nerves badly used and that my bullying would save court martial business. I was astonished later to see him wearing an MC for that engagement.'[1]

Others from the battalion were far more positive, telling of the courage

---

1   Quoted from Robin S Corfield, *Don't Forget Me Cobber: The Battle of Fromelles*, The Miegunyah Press, Carlton, Victoria, 2009, pp. 140 & 314. For a more in-depth account see Bean, *The A.I.F. in France: 1916*, Chs XII & XIII, especially pp.417-8

and skill Murray exhibited when confronted by a ferocious German counter attack. Whatever the truth – the reader needs to be the judge – Murray was subsequently promoted to major and the battalion's second-in-command. Murray's bravery in the face of the enemy was never in doubt when he led his men through more horrendous battles on the Western Front – Bullecourt, Polygon Wood, Anvil Wood, Peronne and Quentin Canal, to name but a few.

After the Armistice, Murray was repatriated back to Australia. When his AIF appointment was finalised, Murray returned to his pre-war employment with the Sydney firm of Anthony Hordern & Sons. In January 1923 he married Madeline Cannon. Not long afterwards he set up his own trucking company. Murray's business expertise soon became apparent – the company flourished and after being named president of the Modern Transportation Federation, the New South Wales state government requested that he take on the role of Chairman of the Transport Advisory Council.

More significantly, Murray kept up his interest in things military. Amongst other appointments he commanded the 53rd and 56th Infantry Battalions (in the Citizen Military Forces) before being promoted to temporary brigadier and command of the 9th Infantry Brigade.

When war came again in 1939 Murray was 47 years of age – an age considered by some to be too old for field command. Yet, again he volunteered his service. After enlisting, he retained his rank of brigadier and, in May 1940, was tasked with putting together the 20th Brigade. Although resources and equipment were scarce, Murray drew on all his military experience, organising training for the raw recruits. While his training techniques may have been hard on the men, and his demand of discipline equally tough, Murray was said to be well liked throughout the brigade. In October 1940 the 20th Brigade left Australia, bound for the Middle East, where the men would complete their training.

The war correspondent, Chester Wilmot, who came across Murray many times, especially after the brigade arrived in the Middle East, and personally liked the man, penned how he was 'a big, genial Irishman who loves a fight. He is ... easy-going but brooks no slackness among his troops and even before Tobruk his brigade was marked out as one of the best-trained in the 2nd

A.I.F. His dogged temperament made him well suited for the defensive tasks that lay ahead.'[2] However, Wilmot was being a little over-kind. It was no secret, among officers and men of the AIF, that Brigadier Leslie Morshead's 18th was the best trained, equipped and most disciplined brigade.

On 9 February 1941, when the 20th Brigade was transferred from the 7th to the 9th Australian Division (commanded by the recently promoted Major General Leslie Morshead) it was still desperately under-trained – particularly in desert warfare – and short of weapons and transport. Barton Maughan recalled how not one battalion in the brigade 'had been issued with its full complement of arms ... [and] the training of the brigades as battle groups had not even begun.' And, it was Morshead – although competently aided by his three brigade commanders, Murray, Arthur Godfrey (24th Brigade) and Ray Tovell (26th Brigade) – who deserves much of the credit for quickly moulding 'these raw units into a division fit for the vital role of frontier defence.'[3]

Murray expected loyalty from his officers and men; and he returned that same loyalty. Morshead had similar traits. Indeed, it was fortunate that the two men bonded extremely well. More so because Murray, as 'senior brigadier,' was called upon to temporary command the division whenever Morshead was called away to a conference or, otherwise, needed to absent himself from divisional headquarters. Certainly Morshead believed in his brigadier's leadership qualities. He would later say of Murray that he was 'a pleasant, forceful character; alert, kindly and cheerful, yet direct and purposeful.'

While the Australians were undergoing further training – now, at least, with some proper weapons and equipment – *Generalleutant* Erwin Rommel's *Afrika Korps* went on the offensive. Morshead's 9th Division was instructed to relieve the 6th Australian Division in Libya. In fact, it was Murray's 20th Brigade which first came up against the might of Rommel's *Afrika Korps* at a little place called Er Regima. Murray and his Australians demonstrated all the resolve and mettle that later would become a by-word among the Axis troops attempting to capture Tobruk. The advancing Germans were held-

---

2   Chester Wilmot, Tobruk 1941, Penguin, Ringwood, Victoria, 1993 (1944), pp.68-9.

3   Barton Maughan, *Tobruk and El Alamein*, Australian War Memorial, Canberra, 1966, pp.10-11.

up long enough by Murray to allow the remainder of the 9th Division to withdraw to Tobruk.

After a succession of victories against British forces in North Africa, Rommel's troops were poised to capture all of Libya and press on to Egypt. All that stood in their way was the strategic port of Tobruk, now garrisoned by Morshead's 9th Australian Division and the 18th Brigade from the 7th Australian Division, aided by a motley collection of units from Britain, India and Poland, including four regiments of British artillery.

What has become known as the siege of Tobruk effectively commenced on 11 April 1941 when Rommel's forces cut off the town on its east (Egyptian) flank. On 14 April the *Afrika Korps,* 'flushed with the fallacy of its own invincibility,'[4] launched the first of its many tank, with supporting infantry, assaults. Significantly, it was Murray's brigade which was largely responsible for repelling the attack. Murray's leadership was such that he was awarded a Bar to add to his DSO.

For 242 days German and Italian forces attempted to seize Tobruk. The defenders successfully fought off numerous Axis attacks and were able to stabilize a front around the town's perimeter. Not only did they repel the ground attacks, but the defending troops had to face the ongoing and largely unopposed attacks from the German *Lutwaffe*. Most frightening were the Stuka dive bombers, with their wailing siren, which inflicted huge casualties on the men stationed in the town, near Tobruk's harbour, where Royal Navy ships were attempting to keep up supplies to the besieged troops.

As 'Weary' Dunlop recounted they also needed to 'endure the cruel extremes of desert heat and cold, and oppressive sandstorms. Their diet is inadequate, water is scarce, dysentery is rife, and their ranks are depleted daily. Morale remains high nonetheless.'[5]

Murray's resolute and clever leadership contributed significantly to the men's high morale and, indeed, the final outcome. His experience of

---

4   E. E. Dunlop, 'Foreward,' in L. Glassop, *We Were The Rats*, Penguin, Ringwood, Victoria, 1991 (1944), p.vii.

5   Dunlop, 'Foreward,' p.viii.

mounting strong night patrols, a technique developed and improved-on during 1918 on the Western Front, proved a bonus. As the siege became more prolonged, the defenders used these patrols to not only keep the enemy off-guard but, more significantly, prevent them from mounting their own reconnaissance patrols from which they could engineer accurate intelligence reports to enable their infantry and armour to strike at the defenders' weakest defences.

Chester Wilmot wrote that the 'measure of the Tobruk patrol successes was indicated by the steps that both the Germans and Italians took to protect themselves. Early in the siege the enemy gave up counter patrolling and stayed behind his defences.' Wilmot thought that 'individually these raids were not of great military importance, but their combined result was to give the Tobruk garrison remarkable freedom of movement, in addition to forcing the enemy on the defensive. He was compelled to waste time, men and material making strong fortifications, and even when these were completed it took at least one German ... division to man them.'

Perhaps more significantly Wilmot believed that 'if it had not been for these raids, Rommel could have left merely a light covering force holding Tobruk. As it was, he had three times as many troops outside it as he had on the Egyptian frontier watching the rising strength of the Eighth Army. As well as tying-up enemy forces, these patrols inflicted not inconsiderable casualties.'[6] For all this success, Murray deserves much of the credit.

Later during the siege (in July and August) Murray was responsible for coming-up with the V for Victory campaign, around the southern sector of the fortress where Italian troops were deployed. Murray ordered that leaflets be printed with '*V Per Vittorio*' emblazoned on them. He further insisted that the leaflets be fastened 'by the use of clips, strings, nails, pins, etc., to enemy bodies, posts, wire, sandbags, etc., by patrols.' As expected, the morale of the Italians deteriorated – more so when Murray ordered that further leaflets be attached to posts inside their defensive positions by his men during night patrols.

---

6   Wilmot, Tobruk, pp.232-3.

By the time that Murray left Tobruk he had been mentioned in dispatches several times. However General Thomas Blamey's reward was somewhat unexpected. Instead of being considered for higher field command, Blamey told Murray that at 49 he was 'unequal to the severe physical trials of modern warfare.' Instead Murray was sent back to Australia to direct the recruiting campaign. However his arrival in Sydney coincided with the Japanese threat, which meant that Murray was appointed commander of Newcastle Covering Force and promoted to major general. Numerous other commands followed – although regrettably for Murray – no combat command.

After the war Murray continued his service to Australia. For three years, between 1946 and 1949, he was Trade Commissioner to New Zealand. This was followed by another two years in a similar role in Ceylon. However his health was rapidly failing. On 8 September 1952, while back home in Sydney, Murray died.

Murray's memoir *I Confess* deserves to be told. Not only does it provide a fresh, first hand – sometimes amusing – account of the siege of Tobruk by a senior officer, but, moreover, it allows the reader to experience Murray's thoughts and philosophy on a wide range of topics; not only soldiering. In his Epilogue his grandson, Andrew, tells how Murray's primary concern was the welfare of the men he led. Though he had somewhat of a distaste for war, Murray always went about his duties diligently. John Joseph Murray was to use that oft quoted expression 'a soldier's soldier.' This book, I believe, is a compelling story – a wonderful tribute not only to a courageous and determined officer but also to those men he led through two world wars.

David Coombes
School of History & Classics
University of Tasmania
Hobart

Studio portrait of John Joseph Murray. WWI period. Michael Hickey collection.

Private H. J. (Harry) Murray (7767), brother of John, joined him in the 53rd Battalion in France in WWI. Barbara Murray collection.

Private T. F. (Fred) Murray (2097), brother of John, killed at Gallipoli 10/11 August 1915. Michael Hickey collection.

Margaret Murray, née Ferrow, mother of John. Barbara Murray collection.

Family portrait pre-WWI. Left to right Fred, Harry, Ettie, Edna, John. Frank and Madge, the two eldest, are missing. Barbara Murray collection.

Lieutenant Thomas
Frederick Hellmrich
(NX33559), nephew of
John, son of Madge,
served as his staff officer
in Northern Australia
during WW2. Amanda
Hickey collection.

Private Edmund
Martin Murray
(1207), first cousin
of John, participated
in the landing at
Gallipoli, 25 April 1915,
WWI. Anita Murray
collection.

Private Patrick Murray (NX102100), nephew of John, son of Harry, in Light Horse uniform, 1941. Barbara Murray collection.

Leading Aircraftsman Denis Murray (164209), nephew of John, son of Harry, in air force uniform WW2. Barbara Murray collection.

Harry Murray is 6th from the right in coat with wounded shoulder. England, WWI. Barbara Murray collection.

John Murray and family leaving for New Zealand as Trade Commissioner, 1946. Right to left: Paul, Madeline, Mary, John, John Michael (born during the Siege of Tobruk), last two unknown. Murray family collection.

John Murray motoring, which was his hobby,
between the wars. Damian Geraghty collection.

John Murray with family between the wars. Left to right: Mary,
Peter, Paul, John, Madeline, Helen. Damien Geraghty collection.

John and wife, Madeline,
between the wars. They were
married 4 January 1924.
John Murray collection.

Wedding of Harry and Rena
Murray with John in the
background. 19 June 1920.
Barbara Murray collection.

Chapter 1

Chapter 1

Fix bayonets, right turn, hat off. The accused, a mere lad of twenty, a soldier of only two days' service, was before me for some small misdemeanour which probably he did not realise was an enormity in the eyes of the great military machine which he had now contacted. The charge was read and, to my question, 'How do you plead?' he replied, 'I don't understand that.' I said, 'Are you guilty or not guilty?' Again came the answer, 'I don't understand that either.' I said, 'Did you do it, or didn't you?' We had established quite friendly relations by this time and he said, 'I did it alright,' and, on my asking in the approved fashion according to the *Army Act*, 'Do you elect to be tried by me or by court martial?' he leant forward and said softly and confidentially, 'If it's all the same to you, we'll let the matter drop.' Well, what could you do?! 'Charge dismissed!' This was one of my proudest moments, for I was able to withhold my mirth until the orderly room was cleared.

These early days at Ingleburn camp in New South Wales (NSW) were truly astonishing. Only the previous night I had driven into the camp unobserved, sitting in the rear seat of my staff car in the dim evening light. The sentry, another two-day-service soldier, arrayed in what was popularly called in those days a 'giggle suit', had stopped the car. To the critical reader, a 'giggle suit' might be described as a shapeless Army creation officially known as trousers and jacket working dress. It was not designed to fit the figure, but to hang around it. The driver, without affording the sentry an opportunity to ask any questions, said, 'Brigadier Murray'. To my amazement, the sentry, pointing in the direction of my quarters, said, 'I think the old bastard lives over in the second hut!'

This was the commencement of the welding into the famous brigade which had the honour to first meet the Germans led by Rommel in this war. These were boys who had left their farms, office desks, factories, the shelter of their homes and the comfort of their families to wage war against an army which, at that time, was the best equipped and most highly trained the world had ever seen. It was those very same men who stopped the progress and played a great part in the final defeat of Rommel and his *Afrika Korps*.

On the outbreak of the present war, I found myself appointed Fortress Commander of Sydney Area. My thoughts at this event went back to those early days of the last war when, as a very young subaltern precariously armed with sword and pistol, I was in supreme command of a half-company stubbornly defending various outposts on the Sydney perimeter. Well I remember the visits of inspection of the Fortress Commander of those days, and the excitement and rehearsals that went on prior to his arrival. Now, in the reverse position, I watched with no little inner amusement those same happenings of twenty-five years ago. On one occasion, while visiting one of the posts, a young subaltern, almost an exact replica of myself in 1914, was taken by surprise. Apparently there had been a celebration the previous evening and various traces of the party were blatantly evident. He got an extremely good 'wigging' from me and it was only two days later, while reading the Sunday paper, that I discovered that the party was a prelude to his marriage. I was to know him later as a major on my staff in the Middle East and told him that, had I known of his impending marriage, I would have made things a lot easier.

I had enlisted for overseas service and, shortly after this incident, was appointed to command a depot training recruits for the 6th Division, a portion of which had already departed on service. This was during my command of the 20th Brigade of the 7th Division. Here you find me at the realisation of my great ambition — in charge of a brigade which would be certain to meet in action the self-same enemy that again threatened our freedom.

The signal announcing my appointment reached me at Ingleburn camp just as we were proceeding to mess. I left the mess that evening far richer in spirit but poorer in pocket. Immediately I announced the news, my brother officers had unanimously fined me nine gallons of beer, in the drinking of which we were nobly assisted by members of nearby messes. The beer was quickly consumed and, not being able to perform the miracle of the loaves and fishes, there was only one thing to do. I immediately selected Lieutenant Colonel F.A. Burrows to command one of the new battalions in the brigade. This produced another nine gallons of the amber fluid.

Burrows, who was affectionately nicknamed 'Bull' on account of his massive build and outsized collars, to say nothing of his almost offensive robustness, was to earn fame later at Benghazi and Tobruk.

I stole out quietly during the festivities to inform my wife of the turn of events. She received the news with ominous quiet. However, I had no misgivings in that direction for we had had many discussions on this matter and, although I realised inwardly that she was consumed with anxiety, I knew that she would accept with fortitude the years of separation that were certain to come.

I did not sleep too well that night. I asked myself whether I was sufficiently equipped and whether I had an adequate knowledge of the work before me. It is a great responsibility handling men's fortunes and lives. Sometimes I thought I had the capacity for anything; but then a couple of instances which I shall recount now completely shattered my ego.

In the last war, just after I had been promoted major, an order was promulgated that saluting officers by other ranks would be strictly adhered to at all times. I passed a private in a small French village who did not salute me, so I ordered him to stop. He came over and I asked him why he didn't salute me. He ostentatiously peered at my epaulette to see the crown and almost leered as he replied, 'I'm terribly sorry, Sir, I thought you were in the Salvation Army.'

The other incident took place in the early days of the campaign in France. I had been sent down from the line to Etaples, on the coast, to deliver a course of lectures on trench warfare. I really believe that the underlying motive of this was that my then Commanding Officer (CO) considered I needed a rest and this was a reasonable excuse. Etaples was a huge depot in those days through which passed all British and Dominion troops returning to their line units, men proceeding to the battle front for the first time, men returning from leave, and those who had recovered from wounds in the hospitals in England. It was a very mixed audience which I had to address. The scene of my first effort took place in what was familiarly termed the 'bull ring'. This might be described as something between a circus and a Roman amphitheatre consisting of tiers of oil drums encircling the poor unfortunate lecturer, who was compelled to speak upwards and in all directions if he were to face the conglomeration of bored countenances which forever gazed down into the pit of despair. Undeterred by these disadvantages, I resolutely thrust my stick into the ground and, with a glance at my watch, hurled my pearls of wisdom at the gathered throng. After half an hour's oratory I asked, 'Are there any questions?' To my extreme embarrassment, an old soldier, an original Anzac returning from hospital, stretched himself lazily and, with a prodigious yawn, said, 'Yes, I've got a question to ask, wassa time?' After I had answered a number of other questions, the same humorist called for the time again and, on my challenging him with 'I've already told you', he replied, 'But this is for another fellow.'

After the mess evening and my restless night, I woke to a new day: a day of bustle, a day of interviews, of organisation and, in addition to the concerns of the organisation of the new brigade, the disposal of my business and the arrangement of my private affairs.

Officers of the 9th Division. Left to right, front row: Brigadier R. A. Thompson, Royal Artillery; Brigadier R. W. Tovell, 26th Brigade; Major General Leslie J. Morshead, 9th Division; Brigadier J. J. Murray, 20th Brigade; Back: Brigadier Slater, Anti-Aircraft Unit; Colonel R. C. Keller; Brigadier G. F. Wooten, 18th Brigade; Brigadier A. H. L. Godfrey, 24th Brigade. Tobruk, 1941. AWM 009525.

Major General L. J. Morshead, General Officer Commanding 9th Division, Tobruk, August 1941. AWM 020347.

Brigadier J. J. Murray with his battalion commanders, Lieutenant Colonels F. A. Burrows (2/13), R. W. Ogle (2/15th) and J. W. Crawford (2/17th). Tobruk, September 1941. AWM 020772.

Captain J. L. A. Kelly (Staff Captain), Major H. T. Allan (Brigade Major), and Brigadier J. J. Murray. Tobruk. September 1941. AWM 020770.

Brigadier J. J. Murray,
Commanding Officer of
20th Infantry Brigade,
Tobruk, September 1941.
AWM 020805.

Brigadier J. J. Murray
finding quiet on the monkey
bridge of the Queen Mary.
Author's photograph.

Officers of 20th Brigade HQ. Left to right, front row: Lieutenant W. Angus, Lieutenant J. R. Watch, Major H. T. Allan, Brigadier J. J. Murray, Captain J. L. A. Kelly, Lieutenant D. D. Halley. Back row: Captain J. B. Blundell, Lieutenant J. H. Elliott, Lieutenant N. B. Trebeck, Lieutenant M. D. Vincent, Lieutenant E. C. Lecky. Tobruk, September 1941. Author's photograph.

Men training at the 'Bull Ring', Etaples, France in 1916. AWM PO2897.003.

Brigadier J. J. Murray and his Liaison Officer, Lt. Ian McMaster on the Queen Mary. Author's photograph.

Officer group between the wars. John Murray is second from left in front row. Mistral Avenue File.

Chapter 2

Chapter 2

Seven years earlier I had set out with a handful of pence to beat the world and formed a transport company. This business was highly personal and I realised that, with my departure overseas, it would not survive. Amongst my correspondence was a request from my bank manager to see him at the bank, a trifling matter of an overdraft. So full of elation was I on entering its portals that I felt as though I owned it, or didn't care who it belonged to. To the conscientious reader a bank might be described as an institution which lends money only to those who have documentary evidence to show that they are not in need of it. At the subsequent interview, when questioned about the overdraft, I replied, 'Well you are a banker and know about these things, could you not fix it up?' I was informed, 'No, it's your overdraft, *you* must fix it up.' In response, I asked, 'Have you ever been in the transport business?' The answer came back a sharp 'No!' but I had the last word: 'You're in it now.' Despite all this, the overdraft was adjusted, but I had had it so many years that even now I feel quite lonely without it.

That was one of the many affairs that beset me, but now I had to concentrate with all the will and vigour that I could command on the formation of the brigade. The recruits began to stream in. I can well imagine their feelings at being pounded on the chest by the doctor, trying to read the bottom line on the eye scales, anxiously awaiting the verdict on their X-rays after two or three days' delay, and then being finally accepted and drafted to the brigade. I realised that it was very necessary for me to select understanding and sympathetic officers to make the first contact and conduct the drafts to camp, for I believe that first impressions are very lasting ones. You can readily imagine that an army hastily got together presented a most unusual spectacle: men with their personal effects in suitcases, biscuit tins, and all manner of containers in which were concealed articles of attire woven by loving, if misguided hands, such as socks, pullovers, scarves and balaclavas, half of which the owners never had the courage to wear during five years of battle, but shamefacedly wore about the house when they were on leave. Personally, I was the recipient of many of these gifts, which I regret to say now lie in the cosy shelter of the bottom of my innumerable cases and chests.

Now began a period of strenuous and unremitting toil — day after day of squad drill, the dull monotony of which has to be experienced to realise just how boring it is. How we longed, every man of us, to emerge from this primary training to the more interesting and spectacular side of soldiering. I recollect on one occasion inspecting the activities of one of the battalions and finding one subaltern in sole charge of his whole company, the remaining officers being in their offices and orderly rooms at divers work. I immediately had them report to me and, after a sharp word or two, told them to spend more time with their men in the field. This incident reached my family in a very curious way. The subaltern was affianced to a friend of my daughter, Mary, and I could not suppress an inward smile on reading a letter from Mary in which she described the incident thus: 'Jean's fiancé thinks you're wonderful! You found him struggling all alone on the parade ground, and you sent out all the other officers to help him.'

I shall brush aside this period of early training and move to that time when we emerged as a trained and equipped force and looked forward eagerly and anxiously to our departure overseas.

We had to move to a country town (Bathurst, NSW) some 136 miles away and, to create a diversion in this wearisome training, I was able to persuade higher authority to permit us to make a staged march by road. In those early days, the press and radio were both anxious for something of news value and this, the longest march attempted by Australian troops in Australia, was something which they were only too ready to glamorise.

This march might sound an extremely arduous task but, in fact, being reduced to easy daily stages, it required much less effort than the parade ground. There is one good story from this trip that sticks in my mind. We rested for one day at a point in the Great Dividing Range, now a famous pleasure resort, through which Wentworth, Lawson and Blaxland had made history 127 years previously. It was not so much a day of rest, but a day of entertainment. A very enthusiastic officer from headquarters (HQ) gathered together a concert party including many celebrated artists. The concert was to take place in the town hall. Just as it was ready to be launched, an excited officer rushed out of the hall to the hotel where we had established my HQ and stammered out, 'All the artists are ready, but there is no audience.' It turned out that the troops were being so hospitably entertained in private homes, public houses and such like that no-one bothered to go along to the concert. At my wits' end I told the officer to bring over to the hotel, *en masse*, the whole concert party to put on their show for the many guests there. This appeared to deliver the party from their unfortunate dilemma. One of the acts was a very diaphanous lady performing a 'skirt' dance, the climax to which was to glide up to and bestow an affectionate kiss on a male member of the audience. I had secretly hoped that I would be selected (she was very beautiful) but she chose Colonel Burrows as the object of her immediate affections. My chagrin was mollified, however, when, after the deed, he looked around in the direction of his wife with what, if he hadn't been a colonel, I might have thought was a guilty expression on his face. His embarrassment completely repaid us for any longing which we might have felt for the glamorous dancer.

And so to Bathurst. We were all relieved to see it, not as you might think because of sore feet — although there were quite a few of us with that affliction caused by dancing, not marching — but in order to enjoy a day's rest after the festivities and fêting which we had received on the journey.

Some little time before, there had come into my life a junior officer who typified to me my ideal of a young Australian. Ian McMaster, who was later to win the MC, be mentioned in despatches and sustain the siege of Tobruk, was my almost constant companion. He was a tall lad, good looking and well mannered, but his chief characteristic was his glorious sense of humour. Another small trait was a wonderful aptitude for falling in and out of love with catlike frequency. Being so close to him, I became the confidant of his, at the time, very serious amours. At first I felt for him in his worries, but afterwards I listened with tongue in cheek to even his most heartbreaking cases. Ian will appear many times in the narrative, but I would like to tell you all something which indicates more than anything else the amusement which we found in each other's company.

I was invited to open a dance in a small country town some twenty miles away and Ian accompanied me. We were received by the Mayor on the porch of what had been a church. He was an old, grey-headed man with a long, drooping moustache. I do not know what his occupation was, but it was my guess that he was the local mortician and this impression grew on me. It added to my discomfort as he mentally appraised us, apparently with a view to future business. After standing there awkwardly for some moments, the mortician Mayor opened his mouth and, having heard of the probable licentiousness of the Army, said, 'What about a drink?' This question needed but little consideration and we were led over a rough, weed-grown path to an empty parsonage, previously hidden in the jungle at the rear of the church.

The occasional table on which reposed a siphon and a bottle of Scotch looked a little pathetic. There was not another article of furniture in the room, not even a chair to share the loneliness of the table. We suitably fortified ourselves for the struggle which was to come, Ian, seeming lost in the aura of gloom, relieved only by joy at my discomfort.

Our mortician also seemed lost for words, apparently believing that his opening broadside of 'What about a drink?' was all he need contribute to the conversation of the evening and, with the resigned air of a man whose duty has been nobly done, preserved a dignified, almost pious, silence. I looked at Ian, but one glance there showed that no inspiration was likely to be forthcoming from that usually sunny countenance. It was up to me. I suggested that we proceed to the dance and was led through a perspiring throng of all ages to a platform which had, at one time, undoubtedly been a choir gallery. What I wanted at this stage was some action and, in desperation, I suggested that I might dance. After another longer silence, the mortician decided that, cost what it might, he would have to speak again, and said, 'No, sit here for a while and let them look at yer.'

We were all set now for a most hilarious evening. I sat there for twenty minutes, the cynosure of all gazes, before I crawled out of my mental apathy and, girding my loins, suggested again that I dance. I had ample opportunity to observe the dancers and, on indicating the lady of my choice to my host, he said, 'No, there is a most influential lady of the district here, and I'd like you to dance with her!' Although I had grave misgivings as to his taste, I decided that I was in the same position as Henry VIII when he made his famous remark, 'The things I've done for England!' My misgivings were more than justified. It was with a feeling of horror that I saw him leading across the floor an apparition of doubtful vintage. At the time I took mental note that I would discipline Ian for laughing at his senior officer when we got back to camp. Has any reader ever danced with a battleship? We came to grips, but got off to a bad start. I placed my arm around her ample and heavily corseted waist and, with futility, attempted to come to grips. The dress that covered the neck-to-knee armour plate was of a particularly slippery material, and I finished at the first pause in the music feeling positively harassed. The open amusement of Ian, who was waltzing around with some beautiful young lass, made me even hotter under the collar. The music started up again and, gritting my teeth, I seized the aged Pavlova and set off feeling as though this was a horrible nightmare, as indeed it was. Succour came to me from a most unexpected quarter. A hand touched me on the shoulder and a voice said, 'Excuse me, Sir, but this is a tap dance.' It was Ian. Bravely shouldering my responsibilities, he took the socialite off my hot and perspiring hands. The dance finished without further event, and the twenty-mile ride back to camp through the cool night air completed a memorable evening.

Our time for embarkation overseas was now fast approaching, and all accommodation in the town of Bathurst had been taken up by wives, fiancées and sweethearts of the soldiers so that they might see their menfolk at every, and any, possible opportunity before they sailed.

The camp being closed for security reasons, six young wives had the brilliant idea of rendezvousing with their husbands at a haystack at the rear of the camp. As you are doubtless aware, the Army has its troubles with regard to women who become professional camp followers for pecuniary gain. I had received a garbled version of the incident, to the effect that some of these women of doubtful morals were attempting to get access to the men in the camp, so I posted a picquet.

The picquet approached these young wives and peremptorily ordered them to proceed on their way, emphasising that if they didn't go, they would put them across their knees and administer a little corporal punishment. The wives were highly indignant at this, and told the picquet that their husbands were in the camp. 'Oh yeah?' was the reply, 'What's their names?' The wives, being unwilling to give their husbands' names in case they got them into trouble, refused to answer and also refused to go. So the picquet took matters in their own hands. One of the picquet, thinking that by some possibility there might have been a miscarriage of justice, asked one of the wives where she came from and she named a certain little country town. It turned out that he came from the same town, and said, 'If there's anything in what you say and you don't want to give your husband's name, tell me your maiden name.' She told him, and he realised the awful truth.

I had to leave the brigade at Bathurst and proceed to the *Queen Mary*, which now lay in the harbour, to be on hand for the embarkation of the 6,000 souls whose home and barrack room she was to become for the next few weeks. Despite all the usual security and secrecy measures relating to news of ships in harbour, I think that everybody in Sydney knew that that famous ship was in. I consider that Mrs Murray must have used her woman's intuition in that she tipped that this was to be the ship on which we would travel. Unknown to me, she and the kiddies had themselves invited by the ship's master to inspect it, and the kiddies succeeded in getting themselves well and truly lost for some considerable time in the myriad passages, corridors and staterooms. Later, I was glad that they had actually seen her, for it made my letter-writing to home far easier. I have never been accused of having any descriptive talent, and the family having seen the ship relieved me of that brow-wrinkling worry.

For security reasons, we tried to slink out of the harbour at ten o'clock on a brilliant, sunny, Sunday morning. This was a very propitious time; there were very few people about — I don't suppose that there were more than 200,000 there at most. All along the bay, the cliffs were dark with waving throngs of relatives, families, sweethearts, newspaper reporters — to say nothing of a large sprinkling of fifth columnists, spies, etc.

I sought solitude, or thought I did, on the monkey bridge which is a kind of superstructure above the ordinary bridge. From it I could see my home in Mosman — it was only a matter of a few hundred yards' distance. I cannot recollect a time when I felt so depressed, so unhappy. I gathered some kind of solace from the looks on the faces all around me. They all looked as if tears were very close, even the most hardbitten countenances.

My feelings on this occasion were very similar to those I experienced when I went to the Great War — only this time the ties of home were stronger. The thought kept recurring to me — 'They can't do this to me again.' Everyone was boisterously subdued, but they all knew the essential necessity for leaving everything which they held most dear, and to do such a good job, no matter how small, that it would help win this war in the shortest possible time to enable them and their loved ones to spend the rest of their lives in untroubled peace.

The harbour was filled with small craft, the most interested, yet doing their best to appear uninterested, that I've ever seen. On one was written 'Goodbye and good luck Brig'. I confess that this homely message helped wonderfully in restoring my spirits.

You have read from more able pens than mine of life on board ship in wartime. I have no intention of attempting to compete with them, but at this stage trouble entered my life in the guise of one Jack Murray, my batman. He could do more wrong in half an hour than any other seven humans could accomplish in a lifetime. He had the appearance of an Adonis with an innocent air but, when the mood seized him, which it did approximately ten times a day, he used his imp of mischief and misappropriation to my consternation and to his personal benefit. At times he had me wondering whether I and not he were the batman. He was loyal to me in his own inimitable way except, of course, when it was contrary to his own sense of humour or pleasure. Ian's father, Sir Frederick McMaster, had presented Ian, Captain Backhouse (another officer of my staff) and me with a case each of Tennant's beer and these reposed in the recesses in our cabins. With my usual generous hospitality any caller was invited to have a drink. You have no secret from your batman, and Murray quickly capitalised on this. Any visiting officer was asked if he desired a drink, mostly when I wasn't there, the drill being that, after one glass, Murray would usher them out and drink the remaining delectable fluid himself. Now Backhouse, who could see when I was out, would make a point of proceeding to my cabin when he knew that I wasn't in, and Murray would pour him out a glass. Both parties seemed very happy over this, the only one who did not take a very good view of it being myself, when I found out about it. I got Murray up before me and stressed that I didn't wish to appear selfish, but surely he realised it was my beer, and that Backhouse was using him for his own benefit. Murray said, 'Oh, that! Don't worry about it. When he goes, I finish off the bottle and sneak around to his cabin, remove a full bottle, put back the empty one in its place in the straw covering, and bring the full one back to you. Any complaints, Sir?'

It occurred to me also that Murray must have had a better stock of completely new garments than any other soldier in the Allied forces. He took particular care not to use any of his own clothes, but wore mine day in and day out. But more of Murray later.

Our first port of call was Bombay where we disembarked and stayed for several days. The men were accommodated inland at Deolali and, before re-embarkation, had some twenty-four hours to spend in Bombay. The British embarkation staff, apparently fearing the reputation of the Australians, actually wanted us to march the men on board the ships where they would remain for the duration of their time in port. It wasn't until we guaranteed the good conduct of our soldiers that we were permitted to keep them ashore, and I was just as proud of them there as always. Never has Bombay had such well-mannered and well-disciplined troops.

Having arranged the disembarkation of the troops, I proceeded to the Taj Mahal, a hotel of great fame, one peculiarity being that it was built back to front. Arriving there in state, I proceeded up the marble stairway and was entranced at having for my private delectation — this word is a new one on me too — the Maharajah's suite. Now I realised for the first time why Indians used black — in fact, ebony — baths, the reason being that they made even my sunburnt torso appear perfectly white. I revelled in that bath and, just as I finished it, there was a rap on the door. Now I was in a perfect dilemma. My dressing gown, I confess, was something between a ragged bath mat and a Venetian blind. Who was at the door? I summoned up my courage and, covering as many holes as possible by assuming an awkward posture, I opened the door. In came an Indian bearer. It is a practice in India for white men, especially travellers, to give letters of recommendation etc. to their itinerant servitors to secure their employment with other white folk. Among others, he handed me a reference which read, 'If you want a man who is strictly loyal, intensely keen, a student of human nature, is very reasonable in his charges, whose integrity and honesty are unquestioned, who is tidy, who is scrupulously clean in his habits, don't employ this bastard.' The British captain who supplied the reference had a fine sense of humour. Irrespective of his credentials, for, in the words of the sages, 'It is always better to employ the devil you know than the devil you don't', his recommendations got him a job.

I then laid me down to sleep, but in burst Ian with 'I have seen the most glorious creature ever. Come and have a look!' It was that same love light in his eyes that I'd seen on some half-dozen prior occasions, and I was not going to become embroiled in any more of his amorous doings. Against my better judgement, I was wakened from my slumberous studies some time later to hear Ian say, 'You'd like her father.' I wasn't very keen about this, but *noblesse oblige*. 'What do you want me to do?' He replied, 'Ring up her father', to which I responded, 'No you don't, young man, if what you are thinking is what I think it is, I'm somehow going to entertain the father while you disappear with the girl. Even Nelson wouldn't expect this of me.' To this day I do not know by what wily speech or entreaties he did it, but he got me on the phone and I arranged dinner that night. The father turned out to be a fine man, an Australian by the name of Prince. His daughter, who, to my surprise matched Ian's description of her, was June. Prince told me a lot of stories at which I laughed — and not for the first time either. We also had mutual friends to discuss. The dinner was going according to plan and, out of the corner of my eye, I noticed Ian slip away with June to the dance floor. It was Casanova at his best. I realised when I saw Ian later that something would have to be done about him. This was really serious. It was love at first sight.

Ian made the best use of every possible opportunity in pursuance of his suit, all military duties being thrown to the four winds. But we had only forty-eight hours in Bombay before our travels began again. With Italy in the war, it was necessary for us to tranship from the *Queen Mary* to smaller craft as it was not worthwhile risking her loss from submarines and aircraft in the Red Sea. I was allocated a berth on a Dutch ship. My first embarrassment was the confusion over the use of the Dutch guilder, especially after my initial sampling of Bol's gin. The journey was uneventful except for a lone Italian aeroplane which paid us a respectful visit — respectful in the distance it kept from us high above the Red Sea. Sunday fell about two days before our arrival at Suez. Mine host, the Dutch Captain, asked if I could help him in preventing the usual souveniring which takes place on board ship. As it was Sunday and there was a muster parade, I took the opportunity to say a few forceful words on this subject before church commenced. Murray, whom I had never heard of attending a church parade before or since, was a spectator because he had heard that I was going to speak. I spoke very firmly on pilfering, souveniring, etc., and must have made mention of some dire penalties. I noticed that, at the church service itself, my worthy batman was nowhere to be seen. On returning to my cabin, one of the staff told me that Murray had rushed down after the muster parade without even waiting for the church service, and, flinging open my own personal sword trunk, yelled, 'Cripes, the Brig fairly went to town about this pinching and I'm not going to be the poor blighter who's going to be caught!' All my belongings in the sword case were hastily thrown out and right on the bottom was a beautiful silver tray — Murray's secret hiding place for his personal souvenir had become the 'hottest place on the boat'. Never before or since have I impressed Murray as I did with my speech that day.

WHERE THE MARCH BEGAN Training scenes at Ingleburn.
Bathurst RSL Sub-Branch Collection.

Early training of 20 Inf Bde was at Ingleburn Camp - from 1 May 40
to 12 Aug 40. Bathurst RSL Sub-Branch Collection.

YOUNGSTERS at Raby school cheered the marchers on.
Bathurst RSL Sub-Branch Collection.

WISE MARCHERS throught first of their feet. One way to ease them.
Bathurst RSL Sub-Branch Collection.

Mock Attacks by R.A.A.F.
planes at Mulgoa gave
realistic A.A. practice to
the marchers. Bathurst
RSL Sub-Branch Collection.

DANGER FROM THE SKIES.
Bathurst RSL Sub-Branch
Collection.

The 2/13 Bn. Mascot ~ he almost "stole the show" Bathurst RSL Sub-Branch Collection.

Another Company at Katoomba ~ a day's well-earned leave ahead. Bathurst RSL Sub-Branch Collection.

March Through Katoomba.
Bathurst RSL Sub-Branch Collection.

Each Group marched through packed streets past Brig. Murray,
who took the salute. Bathurst RSL Sub-Branch Collection.

Over the mountains and on to Wallerawang 20 Aug 40.
Bathurst RSL Sub-Branch Collection.

The first tented bivouac was there ~ but there were
billets too. Bathurst RSL Sub-Branch Collection.

Another Company at Katoomba ~
a day's well-earned leave ahead.
Bathurst RSL Sub-Branch Collection.

Chapter 3

Chapter 3

We eventually berthed at El Kantara in the Suez Canal and were assisted in our entrainment by a number of conducting officers from the main force in Palestine.

One of these officers, a major at that, set out to impress us newcomers, painting a vivid and awful picture of the dangers that lurked in every doorway — of death by natives' hands and of the absolute necessity of being on everlasting guard against the Arabs, the beggars, the thieves, the swindlers and even the animals. I had been there in the last war and realised that this was all ballyhoo, but he evidently so impressed all the others that, even after being put into a camp prepared by our own countrymen so thoughtfully that a meal was ready cooked and the dixies boiling, I still could not sleep that night for the crackle of rifle fire all around me. The men kept shooting at imaginary objects and shadows and finally, in desperation, I had to get one of my officers to quell the noise in order that some sleep could be obtained. There are many of this major's type in the Army and an extraordinary number of credulous soldiers who swallow every word.

Coming to Palestine we were all agog at the thought of visits to Jerusalem and the holy places of which we had first heard at our mothers' knees. On one of my many trips to Jerusalem I visited the Church of All Nations, in the Garden of Gethsemane. I was met by a holy father of the Franciscan Order complete with cowl and hood. I wanted to speak to him, but being a trifle hesitant and uncertain of what approach to make, I finally blurted out, 'Can you speak English?' There was a noticeable pause, and then came the reply —with the nasal intonation of a true nephew of Uncle Sam — 'Waal, I reckon I can say a word or two, I was born in the States.' He was extremely kind and went so far as to permit me to see everything of biblical and theological interest in this garden on which has been centred the thoughts of the whole Christian world for nearly 2,000 years. Thoughts of home were evoked by the wrought iron railing around the high altar which was the Australian contribution to this Church of All Nations.

With the usual Australian perspicacity, the men were buying up on a grand scale what they in their innocence thought was the best value in the way of souvenirs for their loved ones at home that this country could provide, thereby swelling the pockets of Jew and Arab alike. Although this was my second visit to the East, I too fell an easy prey to Ali Baba and his salesmen. I should have known better. In the last war I had been warned to haggle over and beat down any of the company of the above gentlemen. In those days there had been a dressing gown of riotous hue that I coveted and, having beaten the Arab down from 600 piastres to 120, I went back to the mess glowing with pride (I was very young then) at my primary successful venture in the role of buyer in the East. I boasted of my success, only to be offered a similar gown for eighty piastres by other more astute members of the mess. But knowing what I do now, I still consider that it gave its full 120 piastres worth of prize value to my folks at home. One changes as one grows older and, despite the fact that our lads were being robbed right and left from the monetary side, from the point of view of the families to whom the articles were sent, they were worth far more than that price if only from the sentimental standpoint.

One of my proud purchases this time was two pairs of pyjamas said to be the best that a certain millionaire could provide — I found out later that the dark-skinned salesman was referring to Woolworth. I carried these pyjamas with me for many months. I lost the first pair in a pack that fell from the back of a truck in the race from Benghazi to Tobruk. We were too interested in the race to put back for them, but the second pair finished in a blaze of glory. For the first and only time I proudly arrayed myself in pyjamas in Tobruk, we were severely strafed and dive-bombed. When the Stukas had departed and calm was restored, a number of my junior staff held a mock court of enquiry, the finding of which was: 'We find the Brig not guilty of conduct to the prejudice of good order and military discipline, in that he was unaware of the allurement of the beacon in which he was clad, thus causing a Nazi recce plane to pick up our position from a point 500 miles to the north; but the said night attire be burned at the stake.' I had to abide by this decision, for the burning had taken place before the court had made known its decision.

As you can see, my acumen as a buyer of foreign goods resulted in a 100% personal loss to myself and no gain to Australia. Of course, my taste in colours may have had an indirect bearing on this.

It was at this time in Palestine that a world-shattering event took place. I received a letter from my wife to tell me that we were to be blessed with an addition to the Murray family. As you can well imagine, my anxiety was simply colossal. It is not a nice feeling to be away from one's loved ones when trouble is at hand; the home front is of paramount importance to every soldier. I woke the next morning physically ill and my Brigade Major, not knowing the cause, for that is the type of thing that one worries over and cherishes in one's own heart, actually suggested that I spend some time in hospital. On that day I set out for a walk and, after a time, felt rather than saw a little Arab boy of six or seven years of age walking just behind me. I continued on for half a mile or so and discovered him still beside me so, pulling myself out of my reverie, I looked enquiringly at him. He said to me, 'What's the matter, George?' in such a worried tone that I very nearly poured out my heart to him. Instinctively the child knew that there was worry about. However, with the news came many assurances from my wife that everything would be well and this eventually proved more than correct.

To change the subject, the work, training and preparation proceeded so remorselessly that it did not permit the intrusion of one's personal and individual worries although, fortunately, it had its lighter moments. Already arrived at, and arriving in Palestine, were the various medical units with their retinue of Florence Nightingales, and a cup of tea with our own Australian womenfolk was something to be looked forward to and very much appreciated when one had the time to spare from military duties. I recall one very amusing incident. At this time there was a regulation in force that no sister be permitted to ride in a staff car with anyone below the rank of full colonel. One celebrated full colonel who was the CO of the Australian General Hospital (but noted for his untidy and slovenly method of dress) was driving his own car in direct contravention of Army orders. He saw two sisters walking along the road, pulled up and offered them a lift. They turned out to be two reinforcement sisters at his own hospital and, being acquainted with this order but unaware of the driver's identity (he had a pullover on which concealed his rank), said, 'We are not allowed to accept the lift, there's an order about it.' He replied, 'That's alright, I'm a full colonel,' to which they derisively replied, 'That'll be the day, big boy.' The colonel often recounted this tale against himself, but I did not notice any appreciable improvement in his dress.

Soon we were to have a further influx of Australian womenfolk in another branch of the service. The first contingent of VAD girls, each with the honorary rank of an officer, was due to arrive under the command of a Miss McEhlone, whose father I had known in pre-war days in Sydney. We all wished to meet them at the first opportunity and make them welcome in this strange land, so when news of their arrival reached me, I instructed a staff officer to go over to the signal office and send a message to Miss McEhlone stating that I would be free at 1500 hours on that day and asking if I could see her. He went to his task and returned grinning broadly, handing me a copy of the message which read: 'Brigadier Murray will call at the VAD camp at 1500 hours this afternoon, and would like to see Miss Mack alone.' Small corruptions of signals can cause a lot of embarrassment.

Conferences became the order of the day and firing parties and range practices were of increasing importance. After spending a day on the range with Burrow's battalion, I told him to send his car back to camp and to come with me in my car to Tel Aviv for an hour or so before returning. On reaching the city we strolled along the boulevard which faces the Blue Mediterranean. This boulevard was by no means deserted. Men and women of all ages and creeds shared this section of the universe and, among them was a fair sprinkling of beautiful Jewish maidens. One particularly attractive Jewess was pushing a pram and, as we passed her, she said, 'Be quiet, baby.' After continuing on our way for 100 yards or so, Burrows said, 'That's funny — she spoke English.' After making some satirical remark about the dawn of intelligence on a certain officer's mind, I staggered him with, 'And did you notice that the baby was sound asleep?' Colonel Burrows stopped dead in his tracks and half turned around, but it was too late, she had gone. The sequel to this was at a conference some time later. Every one of my colonels was having his say, but Colonel Burrows interrupted the trend of events and switched to a tangent on some great idea of his own which had no relation whatsoever to the matters under discussion. On my 'Be quiet baby', he relapsed into moody silence. I guessed where his thoughts were.

Being particularly interested in sport, not only for its muscle-building aspects, but for its effects on morale, I encouraged the men to take part in sport of all types on every possible occasion. Boxing was, and still is, almost an obsession with me. If there is any tournament in reasonable or, for that matter, unreasonable distance, you would always find me there.

We had challenged the Palestinian Police to boxing matches which they had accepted with alacrity and we had gone to considerable lengths to make them a success. Our best boxers were put into a camp and were properly coached and trained. While I was watching one of these workouts with the Divisional Commander, General Lavarack, a despatch rider arrived in a cloud of dust and rushed to the General with a message, on the outside of which was typed in block letters the word 'IMMEDIATE!' Before the General gave me the 'this is it' look, I had guessed its contents and, on reading the slip of paper which contained our fate, my speculations were dramatically confirmed. It read: 'The 20th Bde will be prepared to move in 24 hours.' 'Where to?' was my first thought, closely followed by the need for preparation for action with regard to getting the units collected. Excusing myself to General Lavarack, I leapt for my car and beat all records back to camp despite the efforts of the Palestinian Police Force to prevent me. I had forgotten all about my driver, who was left witnessing the boxing.

Time was marching on, and I was reminded of an experience from my civilian life. It was Christmas Eve, and my transport business was running hot with orders. The phone would not stop ringing and hopes of spending a quiet Christmas Eve with my family were dwindling fast. The phone rang again, and a voice said, 'This is the Mont De Piete speaking.' In a tired voice, I replied, 'Could you tell me the time by my watch?' I loathe facetiousness in moments of stress myself, but am a great believer in its being applicable to others. The voice spoke again after a pause saying, 'Can you pick up some cases etc.?' 'Oh,' I replied resignedly, 'I thought it might have been that. Well, okay.'

There was a whirr of transport humming through the camp all that evening and night and, next morning, a huge column of vehicles resembling a long black snake could be seen wriggling its way across the Sinai desert. The brigade was off to Libya.

Like a modern John the Baptist, I preceded the column to pave the way. Ultimately we reached Mersa Matruh — the original outpost of the desert, but now far behind the lines of our glorious 6th Division. The opinion held in Cairo at that time was that the war in the desert was over. What an injustice in view of the succeeding months! The first night at Mersa Matruh reminded me of a typical Melbourne Cup day — rain streaming down as we got the men into their bivouac area. We had been informed that the desert was always dry — which, after this burst, proved to be only too true. It was here that a young English officer introduced me to what I thought were two civilians, but they turned out to be two Turkish colonels. The object of these Turks being in the desert was for us to impress them with what we had done and to keep them at least friendly neutrals. They could not speak English, conversation being all in French, which naturally meant that I took very little part. I'm afraid that their French accents varied considerably from my Australian French imbibed from a sixpenny dictionary in the last war in France.

The next day we were on the road again, passing through Bardia and Tobruk en route to Mersa Brega. At Tobruk we experienced our first bombing, a small raid shortly after our arrival. At the time we thought it was tremendous, but later experiences proved it to be very small. I took shelter against the wall of a house by the road which turned out to be the local HQ of the Australian Army Canteens Service. The common danger quickly made us friends and, as the raid petered out, I was invited by the sergeant in charge to purchase the entire stock of liquor. This amounted to four bottles of gin, which I accepted with alacrity.

Tobruk then was but a name on the map to me. I did not realise that it was to be my home for eight arduous and weary months.

We set out again on the road to Benghazi and experienced for the first time the sensation of being bombed in open country by the dreaded Stukas.

One learns quickly from experience, especially when Lethe rides with one.[1] The Stukas usually waited until the column of vehicles had gone over the brow of a hill and, flying low, would come over from behind, strafing and dive-bombing. In the first attack, the padre's car was set on fire and one officer and several soldiers killed because of their lack of experience in knowing when to desert their vehicles and seek ground cover.

We continued on our way to Beda Fomm where, before our arrival, the now famous British 7th Armoured Division had cut off and destroyed a big Italian armoured column. The place was literally covered in shot-up Italian tanks. I understand that, when the Commander of the 7th Armoured Division was told of the Italian position at Beda Fomm, he was a considerable distance away, and that, although his armoured force had sufficient petrol to get him there, there was no possibility of more supplies being made available for his return journey. He made a bold decision and totally annihilated the Italian forces.

And so to Benghazi. It was occupied by Italian civilians who undoubtedly feared molestation from our troops. There is no doubt that, in Axis countries, dictators insidiously sow fear and bestow unenviable reputations on their foes.

While in Cairo I had been given some Italian lira — Italian money being of no value in Egypt. On the first night in Benghazi I was able to entertain my fellow officers at the best hotel with this medium of exchange and receive change from it.

The brigade proceeded to Mersa Brega and, straightway, was given the onerous role of taking over the front line. The Australians at this time were undoubtedly under-equipped but, with true Australian initiative, they picked up various Italian weapons and countless stacks of ammunition which they were only too willing to use against their erstwhile owners. As the men were unused to these guns and the method of firing them, I ordered them to set up targets in the desert — petrol tins and disused drums of all types — for this purpose, and issued an order that a plentiful supply of ammunition be made available for training. One would have thought that battle itself had commenced — guns of all calibres were pouring forth their projectiles into an imaginary enemy.

---

1   Lethe: an obscure term for death used occasionally in Shakespearean texts.

Rommel had arrived with his *Afrika Korps* equipped with the most modern armament and armour and ready for his drive to the Nile. In a very short time the Australians were familiarly versed in the Italian weapons and were prepared for anything that the *Afrika Korps* could offer.

And now we come once again to my incorrigible batman, Murray. I had given him orders to build me a shelter in the desert and, having obtained for him from various sources, sandbags and curved iron, I explained to him one morning how to make it splinter proof and camouflaged. I spent the day on reconnaissance and returned to the position I had designated to Murray to find him spreadeagled on my stretcher on the open desert sound asleep or, should I say, in good Australian idiom, 'passed out'. He was as drunk as he could be. And, before I said anything that I might regret later, I ordered him immediately back to his unit. I watched him buckle up the straps of his equipment to their wrong fasteners, collect all his possession and trudge off disconsolately back through the desert. He cut a comic figure, with a frying pan over one shoulder, his hat awry and looking like a human Thornycroft lorry.

I got myself another batman by the name of Jack Woolhouse who, on sorting out my gear, came across the gin, our sole liquor supply which had been so jealously guarded since we left Tobruk. By now there were only two bottles left. Murray had drunk one and had left a note written in the royal plural saying: 'We have only three bottles left, one of which I am borrowing. I shall replace it in due course.' This was too much for me. I could well imagine Murray's feelings when he faced the morrow with an awful hangover and none of the hair of the dog that bit him to offset it.

At this time there was a secret meeting in a little gully between General Wavell and the field generals, and the decision reached was that, as the British forces had insufficient armour to withstand the force of Rommel's *Afrika Korps* at Mersa Brega, we would have to withdraw by stages to an escarpment overlooking Benghazi. In passing, I might say that Rommel was regarded by the Australians as the outstanding general on the opposing side and was held in great respect by them.

The withdrawal to Benghazi was safely accomplished and General Morshead, the Divisional Commander, placed at my disposal an aircraft — a Lysander — the speed of which was fully eighty miles an hour. It was an artillery spotting plane and, as the Stukas raided us approximately four times per day, I was not too keen, although I realised the necessity of using his gift.

At the first opportunity I rendezvoused with my three battalion commanders at an airstrip, preparatory to making our flight. The plane was very small and I went up first. I found myself facing towards the rear with a machine-gun mounted in my cockpit. The pilot asked me if I knew how to use it. I said, 'Of course,' as I fastened my parachute more firmly and re-adjusted my harness.

At this time there was a story circulating among the troops about an Army paratrooper who was being taken up in a plane for the first time. He left the Army camp and arrived at the 'drome. A flight sergeant met him and said, 'First jump?' and the paratrooper answered, 'Yes.' The flight sergeant said, 'Well, I'll give you a bit of advice. When the pilot says "Jump!" don't jump, but dive, count three and pull the rip cord. If the parachute doesn't open, and they always do open, pull the little cord hanging over your left shoulder. That opens the emergency parachute and you will coast down to the ground and there will be an Army truck waiting to take you back to camp.' When he reached the plane, the pilot said, 'Good morning, first jump?' and the paratrooper answered, 'Yes.' 'Well,' said the pilot, 'I'll give you a bit of advice. When I call "Jump!" don't jump, but dive, count three, and pull the rip cord. If the parachute doesn't open, and they always do open, pull that little cord hanging over your left shoulder. That opens the emergency parachute and you will coast down to the ground and there will be an Army truck waiting to take you back to camp.' The great moment came, the pilot called 'Jump!' and the paratrooper dived out, counted three, pulled the main cord and nothing happened. For a moment he panicked and then, realising that there was the emergency parachute, pulled the cord hanging over his left shoulder. Still nothing happened. He gave it several tugs in desperation and, giving up, called out, 'Just like the bloody Army! I bet there's no truck waiting to take me back to camp!'

Then we flew up this escarpment to Benghazi. My eyes were held between the skies and the ground formation. I must have heard at least forty Stuka engines approach while I was up in the plane. It is wonderful how great a part imagination plays when fear is present. When the plane landed, there was at least one who was not sorry to put his feet on *terra firma* again. The looks of my battalion commanders' faces repaid my discomfort and trepidation as they proceeded sombrely in turn to take their seats for their trip.

Australian infantry occupying Tobruk, January 1941. AWM 005402.

Australian Infantry entering Tobruk, January 1941. AWM 005403.

Italians leaving Tobruk to surrender, January 1941. AWM OO5407.

General view of the town of Benghazi, 1941. AWM OO6175.

British infantry attacking Tobruk. January 1941. AWM 06642.

Italian prisoners at Tobruk. April 1941. AWM 007582.

Wounded soldiers being treated in a field hospital in Egypt, 1942.
AWM 013654.

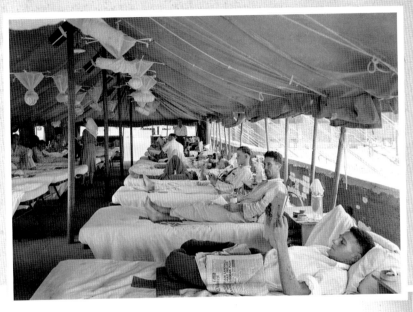

The Tobruk races, 1941. Author's photograph.

Brigadier J. J. Murray
in the Middle East, 1941.
Murray family collection.

A party of Australian
Voluntary Aid
Detachment (VAD)
members, Egypt, 1941.
AWM MED2110.

Chapter 4

Chapter 4

We were several days in this part of Benghazi. The question of the hour was: 'Is this escarpment tank-proof?' and it was finally accepted that, except for the road, it was. A corporal came to me and asked whether I considered it tank-proof and I said, 'Yes.' 'Well,' he replied, 'I'll take you down one part in a utility, Sir.' I said, 'Well, you show me.' So he led the way on foot and I followed in this small truck, with my driver, Hughie Paterson (a son of the famous author Banjo Paterson with whom I had some contact in the last war). It was the most hair-raising experience of my life. The utility seemed literally to hang over precipices and to be continually inclined either way at an angle of forty-five degrees, but we reached the bottom in safety. There we had lunch of dried biscuits and bully beef and beans cooked in our mess tins. I congratulated the corporal and, with Hughie Paterson driving, we finally found the main road.

The next day I received an order to withdraw the brigade and ordered the 2/13th Battalion to cover the withdrawal. The order directed us to proceed back to Barce. I repaired to General Morshead's Divisional HQ and interviewed him. He was drinking a glass of water and he looked at me for a while, finished drinking and said, 'Sit down, John.' I sat down, at the time not having a care in the world. He said, 'I don't know whether you know, but at the moment there are 3,000 enemy infantry and twenty tanks attacking the 2/13th.' I sprang to the phone, got on almost immediately to Colonel Burrows and he said, 'It's all right, Sir, everything is okay. The situation is well in hand. There is nothing for you to worry about whatsoever.' His voice was the voice of a man courteously accepting an invitation to a party. I told him that if he could hold out till after dark I would send transport and would get them all out. Despite the fact that the tanks had broken through his lines, we managed to extricate the 2/13th Battalion and bring the men back to Barce.

I then proceeded to Barce myself. The road was jammed with traffic. I was in a great hurry to get to my new location, but there was one truck and a car in front blocking my way. Hughie Paterson called out to the driver of the truck, 'Move over!' and, from the car, a highly English, Oxford-accented voice was heard to say, 'Move down, McLaughlin, move down.' In fun I often used this remark afterwards with Hughie and it never failed to bring a smile.

The brigade finally took up a position on a rocky escarpment overlooking Barce. From here could be heard the distant crackle of rifle fire which we knew to be the Senussi shooting in cold blood the unfortunate Italian prisoners held in Barce. Brigadier (now General) Stan Savige had told me that he had been compelled to arm a number of Italian prisoners of war so that they might defend themselves against the Senussi.

At Barce we intended to make a stand. Dumps had been set up with stocks of all types of stores, including literally millions of cigarettes. We did not, however, remain there long. Orders came to burn and destroy the stores, but the officer who received the order showed some initiative and allowed the troops to help themselves, which they were not long in doing. All the soldiers took with them as many cigarettes as they could carry. It was not an uncommon sight to see full cartons of them lying by the roadside where they had been cast by soldiers as the load became too heavy. They proved a boon later on in Tobruk when supplies of all types were short. Indeed, I can remember, after five months in Tobruk, a lad standing before me and asking if he could smoke. When I assented, he brought out a cigarette and half-pathetically said, 'This is the very last of the Barce scrounge.'

From Barce we went back to Acroma, a position outside the Tobruk perimeter. I recall an amusing incident in connection with a thermos bomb field discovered shortly after our arrival. The thermos bomb was an ingenious Italian device similar in general appearance to the ordinary thermos flask. These bombs would be dropped in batches from aircraft, the impact with the ground setting their mechanism. They remained there until touched when, with a shattering detonation, the bomb removed all in the immediate vicinity. The approved method of destroying the bomb was to fire at it from a distance with a rifle.

A young officer had been detailed to clean up the bomb field. He had not previously seen this latest death-dealing device and, being a very conscientious type, was desirous of gaining full knowledge of them. With uplifted eyebrows he received the information that it was necessary to sneak up on these bombs, and asked, 'Why sneak? Are they wild bombs?' The reply came back, 'Yes, that's why we have to sneak up on them.' So, moving in a panther-like, Indian stalking style, he and his party commenced their thermos bomb foray. One was sighted and they all went to ground. The officer, fancying himself as a good shot, fired the first round with nil results. More followed, still with the same result. He was truly astonished. 'I couldn't have missed,' thought he and, advancing cautiously, went to investigate. He was surprised at his own marksmanship — three rounds had gone clean through the centre of the thermos, now recognised as one of the ordinary domestic type of flask, not a bomb at all. A thin stream of coffee was dribbling slowly out over the sands of the desert. An irate young British officer appeared from a nearby wadi where he had retired for some purpose of his own, and voluble explanation was necessary from the Australian to explain why he had used the thermos flask for target practice.

We were not, however, to settle at Acroma. Orders were received to return within the perimeter of Tobruk. Hastily summoning my COs, I provided plans for the withdrawal at my palatial HQ, which consisted of a hole in the ground covered with a sheet of canvas.

At this time the ever-efficient and conscientious signals appeared in the form of two signallers with their van and various drums of cable and paraphernalia. Their activities attracted the attention of some Stukas which, forever hovering in the skies like the eagle hawk looking for prey, dived in to attack. Meanwhile, we continued to discuss our plans, oblivious of the impending strafe. Not so the signallers, who were hugging mother earth (the sand). I had not heard machine-gunning from the air at such close quarters before and, not until one of my COs cried, 'We're being machine-gunned!', did I realise that something was on. We hugged the wall of the hole (HQ), which gave little if any protection. The attack ceased, the Stukas without doubt being satisfied with their success. I was not, however, as I arrived at the 'door' of my HQ and was able to survey the result of their handiwork.

Ian McMaster, returning from some mission or other, appeared from the other side of the road, where he had had a grandstand view of the show. Grinning broadly and with a sense of humour typical of all at times like this, he called, 'How did you go?' We were unanimous in reply: 'Not so hot.'

From his 'office' nearby, my staff captain was heard to remark, 'You ought to take a ticket in Tatts. Come and see what they did to me.' According to his description, a portion of the hole in which he was accommodated had been shot away. We excused his description of this physical impossibility which, to the conscientious reader, might be described as extremely good shooting even in those days. We contemplated sending Rommel a message of congratulations on the feat of his men in achieving the impossible. The staff captain was very lucky to escape, and it was he who should have purchased a ticket in the well-known consortium.

We moved that night. This is quite wrong, we moved *all* night, with much cursing and sweating. The blackness of a desert night has to be experienced to be appreciated. If the reader closed his eyes tightly and endeavoured to move about on an expanse of lawn or open space, he would have some idea of how this inkiness almost completely baffled our footsteps. At last we were all within the perimeter of Tobruk, seeking the area in which we were to muster and bivouac. This was easily distinguished being exactly the same as everywhere else — just sand and rock — but, by some very strange coincidence, we found the exact spot. One soldier was heard to ask, 'Is there anything between us and Jerry?' On hearing that there was, he dropped to the sand without removing pack or equipment and, placing head on folded arms, was asleep in a couple of seconds. These boys were tired.

Day dawned to reveal the usual signs that much movement had been effected through the night. Huddled bundles, now perceived as men asleep, began to stir. Miraculously, a meal appeared, not very grand, being the type that a new housewife might produce with a tin opener, but at least sustaining and eagerly consumed. Although not allowed fires during hours of darkness, the cooks had their fires set with material obtained seemingly from nowhere, ready to touch off as soon as they were able without violating the darkness. Hot, scalding tea at these times is not so bad, in fact, it's very good.

Fortified, I called a conference for the purpose of outlining the plan of defence for our sector. By this time a British artillery regiment and machine gun regiment (Northumberland Fusiliers) had joined the brigade. 'Orders' were given — they were quite the pukka type, textbook and all that. At the conclusion I asked the usual, 'Any questions?' and, to my surprise, 'No question' was the stern reply. However, I rose to leave and was instantly mobbed by my COs who each sought to speak privately on all the questions they really did have but which they were a little diffident at putting in front of the others. My answer to the questions, 'Can I do it?', 'Will it work in my area?' etc. was, 'You know as much as I do, now get on the ground and get the "spouts" of your guns pointing in the general direction and, when this has been done, come back and tell me.' They did, and not just a little. By nightfall, all the questions were answered, defences were manned and each had his target. Hard work has its own method of smoothing and solving difficulties. It is a tribute to the courage of the men of the garrison that, despite all that beset us later, every effort of Rommel's failed to dislodge them.

Some days later, on reconnaissance with General Morshead, we found ourselves on what was known as the Green Line, our inner line of defence surrounding the town of Tobruk itself, then but a line on the map. The General said, 'John, if we have to break out, I can find transport for two brigades. Your brigade will be left to man this line.' We both knew that, if this became necessary, the position would be hopeless because of the confined area and we'd surely be ground to pieces by enemy shellfire. I had nothing better to say than, 'That will be nice.' I'd like to deceive the gentle reader that this was courage, but I cannot deceive myself and, to be really frank, that facetious remark was used to cover my prayers (already commenced) that the two outer lines would hold.

On returning to my HQ, I imparted this good news to the Brigade Major, one Major Allan, known as 'Blue' by all and sundry. Standing close behind him was my sometime batman, Jack Murray. 'Where's my gin?' I asked him. That had rankled with me a little and I assuredly needed it at this time. He was not in the slightest degree embarrassed and answered composedly, 'Oh that, Sir, I'll fix that up out of my deferred pay.' He was now 'Blue' Allan's batman. I always had a soft spot for Murray, for when things were toughest, he was always amusing, and was a courageous soldier. But I could see 'Blue' dancing to whatever tune Murray decided to play him. I was very pleased to see him again — I had missed him (as well as some of my personal effects) very badly. I noted with a little satisfaction that Blue Allan's clothes did not fit Murray nearly as well as mine had done. Kindly excuse this facetiousness — you would have to know Murray to appreciate his many sterling qualities — but I was very glad that he was the Major's batman and not mine. Now I could have a chat with him occasionally without that sense of responsibility for myself and my personal effects when he was with me.

Easter was approaching, bringing with it the most determined effort to take Tobruk by the Axis forces. You, as well as I, have read many accounts of this battle. I would not attempt to describe it — it was something that, unless seen, and I could not see the action on the whole of my sector (completely), defies description and is entirely beyond the pen of one puny human. The din was colossal: it rose in an ever-increasing crescendo until one thought one's eardrums would burst. If you can imagine tanks hurling forth their shells; artillery doing likewise; wave after wave of dive-bombers dropping tons of ear-splitting high explosives and the comforting — to my ears anyway — sound of rifle fire; and, above all, a lurid sky suggesting the red blood of brave men, caused by blazing tanks and burning buildings; the huge explosions of burning petrol; to say nothing of the roar of the low-flying aircraft and high revving tanks, you will understand why I fail lamentably to put what is in my heart and mind into words. But what is far harder to describe are my feelings for our men, how proud of them I was: the British tank men in their aged, slow-moving tanks with weak armament pitted against the modern armament and armour of Rommel's Mark IIIs and IVs; our outnumbered gunners, the Royal Horse Artillery — we had practically no aircraft to combat the *Luftwaffe*, only the anti-aircraft units with their red-hot guns — and, above all, those solid and fanatically brave infantrymen who were absolutely invincible in their valour and defied the Axis tanks, artillery, aircraft and infantry so gallantly that no decoration could be high enough for each and every one of them.

My heart even now is over full when I think of them but, as I said in my preface, I can now see a little ray of unconscious humour breaking through. When the heat of battle had only just subsided, a telegram was handed to me. It was from my wife, and read: 'Happy Easter, lots of love, Madeline.' If only she had known!

So arduous, in fact, was our Easter, and so busy our nights, that I was half-dazed with lack of sleep when a German airman whose plane had been shot down and crashed nearby was marched up to me. The Jerry's only wound was a broken arm, but a burst oiling system had covered him from head to foot in oil, so that he looked for all the world like a dripping black beetle.

I was dressed only in an open jacket over an otherwise bare torso, but the prisoner apparently recognised from the gorget patches on my jacket — certainly from nothing else in my appearance — that I was someone in authority and, clicking his heels, he raised his right arm in the approved Nazi salute and solemnly recited the formula, 'Heil Hitler'. In my half-unconscious state I automatically followed suit, raised my own right arm and repeated after him, 'Heil Hitler'. My clerk, who had witnessed this moving scene, was heard to say, 'That was a queer sight. Looked like a couple of blasted Nazis.'

Snatching a very brief, but badly needed rest, I set off to visit the various units. I called on Lieutenant Colonel Crawford whose battalion, the 2/17th, had been in the thickest of the fight. Leaving him, I took what I imagined to be a short cut to my Queensland battalion, the 2/15th. In my party was Hughie Paterson as driver, the Intelligence Officer and, on the running board acting as 'spotter' was none other than Jack Murray. We hadn't proceeded very far when, with a whoop and a cry of 'They're at us!' Murray — as was habitual with him — literally dived for cover (either in a town or in battle he didn't bother to open the car door for me). I am going to deviate a little now. By a freak of coincidence it is exactly four years later to the day that I am writing this, and I am sitting in a comfortable chair in the shade of delightful trees. The day is perfect, and on this tiny promontory, with the gentle waves of the Timor Sea lapping against the shore, I confess that I burst out laughing at the vivid reality of my recollection. Bullets were kicking up dust around the car — with due respects to Tom Mix (I am in good vein today). Despite the door being shut, I had hardly hit the ditch when Murray landed in on top of me. My first thought was that as we were well behind our front line, it must have been some of our own people firing at us in error. After waiting a while we decided to push on, so I told Hughie to get into the car and when we heard the engine start, we would get away in the celebrated Chicago bank-robbing style. Hughie literally sauntered towards the car. I recognised this as pride — I personally would have forgotten pride in those circumstances — and, on hearing the engine revving, we hurled ourselves in and got away to a good start. We had only covered a few hundred yards when fresh machine-gun bursts compelled us to abandon the car again. I could not understand the meaning of this fire at all but, on peering around, noticed at a distance of about half a mile, a platoon of Australians manning a shallow bank and facing in the direction of the machine-gun fire. I watched a tiny figure detach itself from this party and start sprinting in our direction, falling to the ground at every burst of fire from the machine-guns, which were doing their utmost to stop him. As he came closer we recognised a tall, rangy Queenslander, and our surmises proved correct in that he turned out to be a bearer of important news. I told Hughie to whistle him over which he did by placing two fingers in his mouth and emitting a high and shrill blast. I have seen people do this but have never been able to do it myself, despite many dismal efforts. I think it is very clever. The Queenslander made our position in safety, panting so much from his exertions that he could hardly speak. Between gulps he managed to stammer out, 'Lend us yer car, I gotta get an armoured vehicle.' I replied, 'Well, you get your breath first and then we'll find out something.' All he seemed capable of thinking and saying was, 'I gotta get an armoured vehicle — lend us yer car.' In a vain attempt to quieten him, I said, 'I am the Brigadier.' Unintentionally, he paid me a very doubtful compliment, saying, 'I can't help that. I gotta get an armoured car.' I said, 'Right ho, we'll all get into the car and get you your armoured vehicle.' So, adopting our former procedure as Hughie started the car, we made a blind rush for it. As I made for my seat I was closely followed by the soldier. His rifle still had the bayonet affixed and, attempting to get into the car in a flurry of legs, moving car and swinging door, he could not persuade his rifle to enter the car at the vertical. After frantic tuggings, he lowered the rifle, and, drawing it inside, resolutely thrust the bayonet through the roof. He then unfixed the bayonet, dropped it on my toes, and finished sitting on my lap.

We did at last get away, and armoured carriers were soon satisfying the ambition of our friend, the Queenslander. The upshot of this little tale of one private's hardihood was that ninety-eight prisoners were taken. They were a party of Germans who, during the foregoing day/night battle, had passed through our lines and did not know at daybreak that the battle was lost. They were marooned in the old Italian ditch of our second line. This Queenslander is the type of man who is priceless in battle and whose determination to attain his object is completely undeterred by such small fry as machine-guns and brigadiers. The fear of death does not enter his head and he can completely ignore any and all obstacles. In truth, he is the typical Australian man of the line.

German prisoners captured by Australians following an
attack on the Tobruk Garrison. Many 1941. AWM 007475.

Burning German Panzerkampfwagen II. Tobruk. April 1941. AWM 007479.

Men from D Company, 2/13th Battalion,
Tobruk, April 1941. AWM 007480.

Members of a British Army Workshop unit with German tank
captured in the April attack on Tobruk, May 1941. AWM 007576.

Men of the 2/13th Infantry Battalion digging in.
Tobruk, September 1941. AWM 020761.

Two fast Cruiser Mk IV tanks supporting the defence of the Tobruk Garrison, October 1941. AWM 020889.

The Belhamed sector which saw a fierce German tank and infantry attack. Tobruk, December 1941. AWM 022258.

Wrecked German tanks, Tobruk,
December 1941. AWM 022261.

A ration truck of the 2/13th Battalion fleeing enemy fire. Tops of fig
trees can be seen growing around a well. Tobruk, 1941. AWM 128990.

Section of an anti-tank ditch outside Tobruk.
Most ground was too rocky for such a deep trench, 1941.
AWM 134346.

Chapter 5

Chapter 5

The smoke of battle had cleared and all settled down to repair defences, coordinate lines of fire and check all the small details so closely associated with the need to maintain a solid front. All knew Jerry would come again. He did, a month later, with considerable force. I now took a trip along the front to inspect the posts. Some were old and some were new and we had also occupied posts previously used by the Italians in our endeavours to widen the defences.

The troops, having the strong, typically Australian inclination for tea-drinking whenever an opportunity presented itself, were ever ready with their 'Have a cup of tea, Sir.' I readily accepted all this hospitality for it was a friendly gesture on the men's part and I remember on one occasion accepting each and every invitation — the 'bag' for the morning being fourteen cups of tea. This, one might consider as good tea-drinking, even for an Australian.

Shortly after the mammoth tea-drinking effort, an American by the name of Colonel Guy (from the US Diplomatic Corps, I think) paid us a visit. He was an interesting gentleman, well travelled, having been all over the Continent just prior to his call on us. In his desire to obtain local colour, he wanted to get into our front line. I drove him up to the El Adem Road until stopped by a roadblock which really formed a portion of the boundary dividing our possessions from those of the enemy.

The line that morning presented a strange sight. Troops in scattered groups were casually cleaning weapons or performing with equal casualness the ever-necessary chores in the everyday life of a soldier. One instance is well worth a mention. Several soldiers were playing cricket, extemporising with a wooden paling for a bat and a roll of Dannert (concertina) wire as a backstop. The scene was such that one expected to hear the cries of playing children at any moment. Preserving the tranquillity of this glorious April morning, not a shot was heard. Colonel Guy, appearing a little puzzled, said,

'You know, I really want to go to the front line.' With a laugh, I replied, 'You're in it.' He had come prepared to take risks in his search for material and I could almost feel his disappointment. I confess that my comment on the shelling of just a short time before, when 5,700 rounds fell in this sector in twenty-four hours, was but a vain attempt to convince him of the dangers, past and potential. I hope, wherever he may be now, that he does realise we were at the very front.

Listening to an American broadcast some months later, who should be giving the commentary, but Colonel Guy. During the course of his talk he commented on our local paper, 'Dinkum Oil', a single sheet summarising the radio news for the benefit of those without a radio or the opportunity to listen to one. I clearly recall his saying, 'You know, they are great guys out there in Tobruk. They have their own newspaper and call it the "Dinkum Oil", which is Australian slang for the right dope.' This case of the pot calling the kettle black by using this American colloquialism was almost too much for me.

Our activities were not merely confined to hugging the unforgiving breast of the desert, though we were more than flattered by a lot of attention from the air. This really did add that spice to life called variety and I remarked on one occasion when discussing the numerous raids, 'Don't be anxious, it's a good thing. We must be terribly important, you know.'

Eventually we were to become experts in the recognition of aircraft which, at that time, any well-known bookmaker would have laid odds at 100 to 1 on being hostile. My batman, Jack Woolhouse, with the ease born of youth, had developed a sixth sense in this regard and could hear or see a plane long before it was anywhere near the vicinity. He was the proud possessor of a decrepit, battle-scarred pair of binoculars which I had lent him and, during one of his many heaven-sweeping moments, a team of dive-bombers appeared over Tobruk. Being some miles to our rear, we felt we saw in someone else's misfortune something not entirely displeasing to ourselves. However, to continue, Jack was giving a ball to ball, or should I say bomb to bomb and plane by plane, description of the raid, and I asked, 'What do you make of them, Jack?' The reply was almost a classic: 'I think they must be Itis,' he said, 'one of the cows is diving upwards.' The Italians were certainly the butt of many a piece of humour.

With due regard to all the humourists to be found in the brigade, one Joe Blundell could be described as the brigade wit and his rare brand of humour was a tonic. The reader will now remember him as the dashing young subaltern mentioned earlier when gallantly assisting me in the defence of Sydney. By this time he had become a major with the 2/17th Battalion.

Because of losses from casualties, I had occasion to call him into Brigade HQ as a liaison officer (LO) and one of his first duties was to take a message from me to his own unit for Lieutenant Colonel Crawford and bring back such information or requirements from him as would be the concern of the moment.

Joe, now using his position as a 'powerful official' from the mighty Brigade HQ when making this visit, couldn't resist a call on his pals in the line. His description of the duties of a LO which, by the way I received back by bush telegraph (an absolute miracle since there was no bush — I suspect the underground) was indeed amusing. Naturally, his friends had hailed him with 'What's it like being at Brigade HQ, Joe?' 'Well,' said Joe with his inimitable sense of humour, 'it's not bad. The Brig comes out and says, "Listen, Blundell" (or "Joe", depending completely on his humour at the time), "I want you to go up to the 2/17th Battalion, tell Lieutenant Colonel Crawford so and so and bring back any observations or information etc. of import." I listen very carefully, of course, both eyes well open and my mouth closed until the appropriate moment, and then say to the Brig, "Are you going to handle this job or will I do it?" If it so happens that I am in his favour at the moment he says, "No, you fix it up, Joe," so now I am up here to tell you where you get off.'

It was by such men as Joe Blundell with their wonderful, sometimes unconscious humour and wit, that a hitching rail was provided for the bored minds and tortured nerves that existed during the many weary months of our static garrison duty.

Around this time we re-sited the HQ. This, of course, meant rebuilding our 'dingus' (no plural), the built-up cairns of stones that served, for the purpose of the exercise, as 'offices' and such like. There was great competition amongst all concerned to see who could produce the most elaborate 'dingus', camouflage in those times being of paramount importance. As luck, fate, or my decision on the siting would have it, the area had once been a rubbish tip. The staff captain thought we ought to preserve the appearance of the place and let it continue to look like one. I was all for having it cleaned up, but the Brigade Major said, 'Let's pour the rubbish over each dingus.' Eventually this happened and all were happy. Not so happy were we when, on returning from a day out on the ground, we found that a young, very enthusiastic officer of the day, deciding that the odd sardine tin shining in the sun would attract the seeking eyes of our ever-present enemy, the Stuka, had the whole rubbish heap removed. It was a blow, and effectively ended the one-act play titled 'The Camouflage of Brigade HQ'. How humorous these seemingly trivial matters appear in retrospect.

The daily life of a soldier is far different from the popular conception. Most of the worries and anxieties of soldiering occur at night and, after 'stand to', that hour before dawn which seems like a day, it was customary to snatch a few hours' sleep on top of a meal of bully beef and biscuits which all the skill of the cooks couldn't disguise.

My batman had produced, as usual from nowhere, a sign inscribed, 'Please don't disturb', this warning being hung in the portals of my 'dingus'. At that time, General Morshead was a frequent visitor to my HQ and, uncannily, made his visits when the sign, like that of 'Stop! Look! And listen!' shouted forth its warning from a conspicuous position. I had suitably impressed the staff to treat this sign with absolute respect, but despite the fact that the General would say, 'If he's tired, let him sleep', I cannot remember an occasion on which I was not woken. The staff would be delighted to do this, and have a clear conscience doing so.

At this time, mail was arriving and naturally was eagerly sought by all ranks. The silence which reigned after its distribution was supreme, as each one of us, seeking our respective lairs, was hushed by this great event. All manner of news from home was devoured. It was on one of these occasions that Ian appeared flourishing a letter and crying, 'I have a letter from June' — remember that glorious creature in Bombay? 'I take a very dim view of it, too. Half the letter is about you.' I guess I didn't figure among the interesting comment of the well-known sporting page.

Although to us the arrival of mail, no matter how frequent, brought ever fresh delight, it was not so with the Polish soldiers, a brigade of whom joined us later. I remember the pathetic scene among these fellows at the time of the mail call. Most of them had not had news of mothers, wives, sweethearts and others of their families for two years. I believe our excitement unwittingly, perhaps, served to sting the wound in the hearts of these brave men.

Life, of course, went on and one of our biggest domestic problems was that of cooking, a sheer impossibility on a unit basis. Section cooking, where each post catered for itself, became the order of the day and, despite the lack of any previous experience, the members of these sections soon became experts in the culinary art.

On one of my visits to the 2/15th Battalion, Lieutenant Colonel Ogle, the CO, appeared with the self-satisfied look of the man who has dined very well. He was not long in telling me that he had just finished the best meal he had ever had the pleasure of eating in Libya. Good and all as our cooks had become in the feat of food camouflage, this seemed rather strange, but it appeared that on one of his numerous visits to his posts he had come across a section which took more than just pride in the preparation and serving of their food. It was an honour to them. Dishes containing bully beef fritters, pineapple fritters, and macaroni cheese (so thoughtfully provided by the Italians) had an appearance calculated to make even the driest of mouths water. The CO couldn't help remarking on this and said, 'That looks very appetising,' and his troops, not missing a chance of getting 'big' with the 'old man', replied, 'What about having lunch with us, Sir?' He did, squatting down in the little trench to do so.

Long after, when we were relieved, this incident had its sequel in Palestine in the city of Tel Aviv. Colonel Ogle sent a message that this section would report to him for special duty at the 'Hotel Gatremon'. A utility had been ordered and placed at the section's disposal. Thoughts were rioting through the minds of these soldiers: 'What on earth can this special duty be?' and great was their confusion and stammering when, ushered into a specially prepared room at the hotel, they were received by their CO, now commanding a table literally groaning with the weight of victuals. The nature of the special duty was obvious, but the troops still couldn't grasp the situation. Colonel Ogle was not long, however, in explaining his motive and, with the ease of one of nature's gentlemen, soon removed any traces of embarrassment felt by 'his boys'. Lunch finished as a roaring success. This fine act was so typical of the relations that existed between COs and subordinates that it could not escape mention in this narrative.

The officers of Brigade HQ had a treasured possession in the shape of a battered, dilapidated gramophone which, incidentally, 'Blue' Allan of the mechanical mind, insisted on pulling to pieces almost daily, allegedly for the removal of sand. We suspected that he did it more because he just loved doing it. Were we right, 'Blue'? Records, of course,were terribly scarce and everybody was continually on the 'scrounge', even in the most unlikely places. In the course of time, some marauding tactics produced, unbeknown to me, a new record which they thought would be something appropriate to play after I had risen from my frequent brief slumbers. Its introduction for this purpose was quite novel.

After the activities of the night and the usual morning 'stand to', I had retired to the 'castle' for the ever-needed forty winks. On rising from these slumbers, I repaired to the mess, so called as it was nothing but a heap of sandbags and stones, for a cup of tea. Several of my young braves were there and, after the customary morning greetings, someone enquired if I would like to hear a new record. My 'yes' was proved rather hasty in the light of what followed — they played 'Little Man You've Had a Busy Day'. However, humour, records and myself, an unbroken trio, did not end there.

Again it became necessary to call on the battalions for another LO for Brigade HQ staff. This time a Lieutenant Bayne Geikie, a man of immense stature, was the unfortunate. He is, at the moment of writing, a major fighting in Bougainville. Those bright, practical-joking commandos of my HQ as usual gave the newcomer a welcome of mixed parts, included amongst which was a distorted version of my characteristics.

At Bayne's first breakfast, a meal of the everlasting daily horror, bully beef, which was fried in batter in a vain attempt to disguise it, I said, looking at him, 'Geikie, you are nearest to the gramophone, slip on a record.' He did this with as much speed as his bulk would permit. I expected something bright and, to my surprise, out broke the strains of 'The Lost Chord'.

I was to learn later that Bayne had been advised by his new messmates, 'If you want to get in good with the "old man"' (I resented the 'old'), 'be sure you play "The Lost Chord" if he asks you to put a record on, it's his favourite.' Remembrance of his speed at the breakfast was now significant to me. There was much laughter at the breakfast incident after I had left as Bayne was acquainted with the oddity of what he had done. He seized the record and smashed it on the head of the nearest, which only goes to show how 'The Lost Chord' became lost.

I cannot resist, at this stage, making further mention of Lieutenant Colonel Ogle, whose position was now overlooked by the Germans. Jerry had come again as prophesied and captured a feature (not on my front I may say with some pride) that dominated our sector. He seemed to be able to peer right into our private lives — a most embarrassing situation, as you can well imagine.

It became necessary again to visit Ogle's HQ, another hole in the desert thinly protected by stone and iron, and, with utter disregard for the necessary precautions, I drove up to this elaborate construction in a cloud of dust, feeling secure in the belief that this would hardly be distinguished among all the other dust clouds. I didn't reckon, apparently, on the extraordinary powers of perception of our very unfriendly enemy. They commenced shelling us, I suppose not unnaturally, but nonetheless it surprised me in view of my earlier brilliant thought. Bob Ogle's look, for which I never forgave him easily, was eloquent with the expression, 'Now see what we have to put up with' as, at moments like these, the naked truth shines out. I might say I wasn't feeling too comfortable myself, and adopted a running position very smartly, this time in the direction of the phone. I got an immediate response from my colonel of artillery, Lieutenant Colonel Williams, CO 1st Royal Horse Artillery, the right of the British line. He was an excellent CO, soldier and gentleman, with a very fine regiment. When I had outlined my predicament, he cheerily replied, 'I'll fix them.' I swear he said it with a chuckle. 'I'll put the whole regiment on.' It was but a matter of seconds before the roar of his 25-pounders — twenty-four guns in all — commenced. Jerry was quickly silenced. My satisfaction at the double success was tremendous. You see, I had evened scores with Bob Ogle, too. I thought it was now decent to leave and, sauntering insolently to my car, stepped in and drove away.

Incidents of this kind were an almost daily affair — it was certainly a hit, duck and run war. We couldn't run far, however! There were no rules, of course, and every game had a slightly different form, no less nerve-wracking and exhausting than the one before. They also had their humour afterwards — in spite of their near tragedy — and I cannot pass at this stage a story which had all these properties.

On a visit to the other brigade areas with Major General Morshead (I was then senior brigadier in the garrison and virtually Deputy Divisional Commander), we called on the commander of the brigade on my left, Brigadier Arthur Godfrey, who later died gloriously leading his brigade in the battle at El Alamein. We were old friends from the last war when, as an inconspicuous junior officer, I served in the brigade of which he was staff captain.

After some discussion, we strolled up out of the wadi which served as his HQ. Everything seemed peaceful enough when, I'm afraid to the secret delight of everybody in view, a plane came screeching down out of the skies. It seemed literally to stand on its nose on our headgear. My facility for seeking cover in a space of moments was phenomenal and born of long association with the need for this practice. I outpaced the General and Arthur to a nearby rock, finishing streets ahead (pardon the exaggeration and the absolute impossibility — we had no streets). Fortunately, the plane dropped its bomb a hundred yards distant so, shaking the dust from our attire, we resumed the walk.

One's thoughts in the fleeting moments during such situations are purely personal and I considered that the attack had been directed at me, although on reflection and thinking of the red-banded caps present, I decided that it was an attempt to wipe out the 'divisional brains trust' (I'm being facetious again). However, the thought didn't end there, as I said to the others, 'Do you realise that my right-hand neighbour, Brigadier Tovell, would be Divisional Commander if the attack had been successful?' This remark, unhappy though its portent may have been, was sufficient to restore each of us to reality and the incident was closed.

Thought of my own fleetness of foot on these occasions revived memories of an incident during the almost-forgotten Battle of Peronne, 1 September 1918. I was a company commander and had reached an objective which was not where I was supposed to be — quite silly, of course, but perfectly natural under the circumstances. COs being rather interested in this sort of thing, I made haste to despatch a message informing mine of the situation. The message was given to a runner with most explicit and careful instructions concerning the route he must take in order that his safe arrival at Battalion HQ would be assured. He was to proceed through a cemetery, a wood, and then down the main Peronne Road and, on no account, to take the direct route, since the area in our immediate vicinity was being shelled heavily. He just couldn't miss and the message was delivered, but my influence ceased here and he decided to return via the short cut through the shelled area. I have no doubt that he regretted this as it happened because, when he reached me (strangely enough in one piece), he breathlessly stammered out, 'W-what t-time did you s-say P-Postle [the famous runner of the day] did the 100 yards in?' I replied, '9 7/10 seconds. Why?' With flippant disregard for probabilities and possibilities, he replied, 'Well, I've just cut off the 9.'

I have digressed again — a pardonable sin, I hope. Tobruk cannot be dismissed without mention of the bush artillery. Weird and wonderful were the tactics of these odds and ends — cooks, spare batmen and so on — with their captured 75mm Italian guns, and it was not uncommon to hear range corrections given like the following orders: 'Cock her up on some rocks, Joe, to give her a bit more range' or, 'Swing her off to the right two telegraph poles.' Our regular gunners were interested, besides being most envious of the unlimited supplies of captured ammunition compared with their own carefully rationed shells and, with their assistance, the improvised gunners became quite expert, though they never lost their individuality.

I arrived unexpectedly at their battery site about noon one day to find all but the sentries had gone to earth. When finally the young officer in charge appeared, I learned the reason: 'They've been firing since early morning, Sir, and are all resting now, but they'd be terribly disappointed if they couldn't put on a "demo" [demonstration] for you.' I was not particularly thrilled by the suggestion, knowing that the fire of these enthusiasts would be sure to draw a corresponding answer from the enemy, but I couldn't disappoint them, and it was interesting to watch the professional way the battery was handled. 'Stand to!' shouted the sergeant into the megaphone in stentorian tones and, from the holes and shelters rushed the men to man their guns — they really thought an attack was on. 'From the right, one round gunfire at one minute intervals,' yelled the sergeant. Then, from the young officer, forgetting for the moment his professional status, 'Give us some quick stuff, sergeant.' 'Five rounds gunfire,' yelled the sergeant, equally enthusiastic, though managing to retain something of his dignity as a gunner.

I admired the 'demo', made some suitable remark, and resumed my journey, comforted to know that I was well out of range of retaliation when I heard the sounds of the inevitable German counter-battery fire.

Colonel F. A. Burrows (2/13th) examining a captured tank.
Tobruk, April 1941. AWM 007468.

Outer defences of Tobruk with a Bren gun post on the
El Adem Road. April 1941. AWM 007470.

Bakers removing bread from 'Aldershot' ovens in the field. Tobruk, May 1941. AWM 007521.

Printing the 'Tobruk Truth', a one sheet daily news summary. Tobruk, May 1941 AWM 007581.

A gun crew in action. Tobruk, September 1941. AWM 009958.

Lieutenant Colonel J. W. Crawford outside his headquarters in the El Adem sector. Tobruk. September 1941. AWM 020205.

The 'bush artillery': men of the 2/17th Infantry Battalion using a
captured Italian 75 mm field gun. Tobruk, September 1941. AWM020277.

Camouflaged quarters
of Major General
L. J. Morshead. Tobruk,
August 1941.
AWM 020288.

Cooks, orderlies and drivers of the 'bush artillery' harassing the enemy for the fun of it. Tobruk, 1941. AWM 040615.

Sappers of the Royal Australian Engineers preparing defences with a jack hammer. Tobruk, 1941. AWM 040623.

Chapter 6

Chapter 6

A brigade of Poles began to arrive to relieve our 18th Brigade under Brigadier (now Major General) Wootten. The Polish Brigade was not supposed to be in Tobruk (weren't they unlucky) but, perforce of circumstance, had become involved in the quarrel with Rommel and Co. — some quarrel, believe me. We were very anxious to welcome the Poles cordially, but one can readily understand that, as the language difficulty was considerable, and as all the ins and outs of movements in this matter obviously had to be carried out at night, this didn't add up to make the task of the reception group an envious one or the welcome a smashing success.

One Major Bert Locke (poor, unfortunate chap) had the onerous task of meeting the arrivals and conducting them to their staging area, another of those pieces of sand and rock cast about with reckless abandon over the desert.

The main drill established for identification purposes was to poke your head in the back of each truck as it left the shipside and ask, 'Anybody here speak English?' Conversation would then follow on the lines directed by the nationality of the person replying. Even the best-laid plans (you know the rest) — and I'm afraid this didn't work quite as effectively as had been fondly imagined it would. Bert, bailing up one vehicle and making the usual query in the approved manner, received from the dark interior this reply in the unmistakable tones of an Australian (a prickly customer), 'What in the — hell do you think we speak?' They were some reinforcements for my own brigade. How fortunate were they.

Reinforcements always provided us with a joke or two in their innocence (or ignorance), and no less amusing than many other stories told of them is one of a soldier joining his section. It is necessary to mention here that reinforcements, having disembarked, were given a day's rest at the staging camp where detailed arrangements took place for their allotment, right down to the section of the unit to which they would belong henceforth, come hell or high water.

All movement, you must appreciate, took place during hours of darkness. On the night following his disembarkation, one lone reinforcement for a section of Lieutenant Colonel Burrows' battalion trudged on his way. After much exertion he eventually arrived, still in the dark in more ways than one, as you will see. Unbeknown to him the section had been ordered on patrol and the troop joined the group of men now moving on the corporal's 'Come on, fellows.'

Unsuspecting, the reinforcement plodded on, still complete with all his regalia, no doubt imagining the journey as but another stage in the already long and arduous business of joining a unit. Not having realised the necessity for quietness, the noise of his progress resembled that of a hardware store rolling along and knocking stones out of its way.

The corporal (slightly incensed) in an Irish whisper ordered, 'More quiet back there.' This seemed to encourage the reinforcement who, after all, had had a long trek, because he asked, 'How far is this — front line?' 'Front line?' queried the corporal, 'Why, you're just a thousand yards in front of it.' The soldier's disgust was supreme.

Now we must return to our Polish friends who, having settled themselves domestically, had begun to be most aggressive, a worthy attitude. They had every reason to hate the German. Their one aim was to kill as many of the enemy as possible with little regard for their own or anybody else's safety. It was not uncommon to find, on relieving them, minefields uprooted and sown in an irregular criss-cross pattern, or other traps of this sort laid in the hope of catching an unwary German or two. It was positively harassing and not just a little disconcerting, as we had to be just as wary as Jerry. I personally proceeded with the utmost care over any sector recently occupied by them. Tales of their desire to get at the Hun are legend and it didn't stop at setting Jerry traps or some fiendish plot for ridding the world of some more pure-blooded Aryans.

Our artillery, though greatly outnumbered, was not lacking in spirit either. Enthusiastic forward observation officers found great sport in 'knocking off' single trucks — in fact, any single thing within range became an 'Aunt Sally'.[2] It can be imagined the drain this posed on our meagre stocks of ammunition, strictly rationed owing to lack of supplies caused by the shipping shortage. The ration per day was fixed at ten rounds per gun, and was not to be exceeded unless in exceptional circumstances.

Imagine our bewilderment, after the Polish boys took over, when faced with the problem of dealing in a disciplinary manner with those Poles found to be stealing shells from the ammunition dump. I was nonplussed. Food, liquor, etc. — yes, quite understandable and easily fixed. But this was the only occasion I ever heard of soldiers 'scrounging' from ammunition dumps.

I regret to say that we did have to deal with those troops. They were so eager it was a pity. Normally they would have used their whole day's ration of shells before breakfast and the rest of the day would be spent borrowing ammunition from all and sundry about them, not to mention the marauding efforts connected with the dumps. Their enthusiasm was pathetic. This was the first occasion on which they were able to face the German since the year before and they meant to even scores with him as soon as possible. More on Hitler's best haters later.

The 12th of June 1941 dawned — with deep apology to my readers' already overtaxed patience — an epoch-making day in my career. John Michael first saw the light of day, and a cable from home assuring me that all was well put me in great heart. He was the fifth child of our marriage and I'd always harboured a secret longing for a son named Michael.

News of such important events quickly spreads and the telephone wires positively sizzled with rings for me and with my ringing to tell others. I fear the signaller at the switchboard became rather fed up with all this additional traffic and was swearing roundly when I happened to pick up the phone. An odd baby or two arriving in the world hadn't stirred his paternal spirit. However, I spoke to him rather crossly and said, 'Do you know who you are

---

2   Wartime slang for an easy target.

speaking to?' Surprised, he replied, 'No.' 'Well,' (seeking to impress him) 'it's the Brigadier,' I said. 'Oh,' came back the Sig, 'do you know who *you* are speaking to?' 'No,' said I, and he was heard to gasp, 'Thank God!'

Leave was ever-present in our minds, but was a practical impossibility. However, no soldier, be he general or private, ever gives up a secret hope that, by some strange freak of fortune, he may be granted leave. I consider that there were more rumours about leave in this war than about Hitler's demise.

With this myth in mind and having in some deep recess of our hearts the thought of the sign at Eagle Corner which read, '9,999 miles to Griffiths Bros.' (a well-known Sydney firm famous for its advertisements spaced along suburban railways which read, 'XXX miles to Griffiths Bros.' according to the actual distance), the reader will understand the impishness with which we attempted to convince ourselves that we might eventually arrive in our families' arms. Realising that Tobruk was the only place in the world that was fighting the all-conquering Hun, I am amazed at our insolence in daring to think as we did. France and practically all Europe had fallen and, as everyone knows, Russia and the USA were not at that time participants in the world struggle. I wanted that one freak of fortune that I have referred to previously — something similar to a secret weapon that would win the war for us, and which we in our hearts always hoped for — in order that I could get back home on leave. I distinctly remember saying to another officer, 'All I want from this war is that I fight my greatest battle at home. I'd give anything to be with my mate having a battle on the home front at this present moment.' I did tell my wife on one occasion in a spirit of fun that the wedding march was the greatest battle song ever written. Only Ripley could tell whether she believed me or not.

In Tobruk at this time was a member of the protective platoon that performed the function of guarding my HQ. He was known as 'Little Tich'. I cannot ever recollect him being referred to by any other title. Suffice to say, the name suited him to perfection. He was about five feet two inches in height and his small face was adorned with a huge, bristling moustache. On top of his soldierly duties, he was the HQ hairdresser.

When I resorted to his tonsorial art we developed a short period of mutual understanding. In true barber's style he barraged me with questions: 'Nice day, Sir. Do you think Jerry will be over today? Will Turkey come in?' etc., and then he asked me how I'd like my hair cut. 'In silence,' was my reply. Silence reigned for a short time and then came a hushed tentative question, 'Would you like it cut or trimmed?' We were friends. I said, 'Why the odd question?' to which he naïvely replied, 'Well, Sir, the boys asked me to ask you that. They reckon that if you are getting it trimmed, we'll be getting out of here pretty soon [there was a big rumour that a relief force was coming up from the south], but if you want it cut, we'll be here for the duration.' I asked for a trim, not that I had any hopes at all in that direction, but one never knows. Besides, it helped my own morale.

Glancing back over the pages already written, it occurs to me I may have conveyed the impression that the course of events has been dealt with somewhat light-heartedly. One, however, was always conscious of the ever-present danger to and the valour of our men, the Australian and British alike. Striking a serious note, this, I think, is clearly voiced in the following broadcast which I made in Tobruk. To me it is more expressive of my feelings then than now as I write these lines four years later:

> Here in Tobruk we've just learnt that the Commonwealth Government is raising another war loan. This time it's for a hundred million pounds. That's a lot of money, but we've got to find it somehow. We're fighting an enemy who has staked everything on this war and who's forcing his own people and those he's conquered to make severe sacrifices in the hope of victory. We don't think for a moment that he will win. For six months in Tobruk we have been fighting the Germans and Italians and we know they're not good enough to win, provided our men have anything like a fair chance. But before we are sure of winning, we must make the same sacrifices as the enemy has made. Nothing short of complete national effort can bring us victory. Half-measures are no good, and the sooner we stop thinking that they are, the better. As Australians we're inclined to be satisfied with 'that'll do' or 'that's good enough' — but that standard won't do. Nothing will do short of what has been called the 'Tobruk Standard'.

I think I can talk about the 'Tobruk Standard' because I have the honour to command the infantry brigade which has been longest in Libya. The men under my command have helped to set the 'Tobruk Standard', and I'd like to tell you the kind of standard they've set.

They've been courageous and self-sacrificing — they wouldn't be good Australians or good Britishers if they hadn't been. But they've set a standard of cool courage that kindles memories of the Anzacs. Take this case: one Easter Monday the Germans attacked us with all their power. They were repulsed. You probably know the story of that repulse. But even so, it's worth repeating two things. During the night, about fifty Germans were met in no man's land by an officer, a corporal and five men. Our small party, without hesitation, charged with the bayonet, killing many Germans and compelling the remainder to retire in disorder. It was one of the most gallant things I've seen or heard in two wars. The corporal was Jack Edmondson. He was awarded the VC. Later, when the German tanks penetrated our line or perimeter posts, the infantry held their ground and, by so doing, they were able to beat off the German infantry attack which followed the tank attack. No infantry had ever done this before, and the Germans couldn't understand the courage of men who kept on fighting after their posts had been overrun by tanks. This sticking power, this refusal to give way, no matter how black the outlook — this has saved Tobruk.

Then they've shown another kind of courage — the daring, almost brazen initiative which had led parties of half a dozen or so to storm enemy strongposts or engage enemy patrols. Here is a case: some two miles outside our defences there was an Italian strongpost held by about fifty men. They had a number of machine-guns and anti-tank guns and were protected by mines, barbed wire and booby traps. An officer and ten men raided this post and killed at least fifteen and wounded many more. They crawled through the wire and the booby traps and they charged the post from the rear. One sergeant, a slight lad of twenty-one, killed or wounded at least five Italians himself, and even in the heat of the struggle had the presence of mind to stop and search his victims for tell-tale papers. The patrol leader was wounded as he went in, but that didn't stop him. He was determined to get a prisoner and, at one stage, he had two Italians by the scruffs of their necks trying to drag them from a trench. He only let them go when a hand grenade burst right in front of him and wounded him again. But he led his patrol back and sang as he came in.

I could talk for hours about instances like this one, but the men of Tobruk have needed more than courage. They've needed that optimism for which Australians are famed. In the early days here they saw our airmen shot out of the sky, overwhelmed by sheer numbers. Then they were dive-bombed almost with impunity and they couldn't hit back. They've seen enemy tanks in fifties and sixties and our own tanks in fives and sixes. They've been at the receiving end when heavy German mortars have been in action and they've had nothing to answer with. But what did they do? Did they throw in the towel? Did they say, 'We can't carry on in conditions like these. We must have this and that before we will fight?' Certainly not. They just gritted their teeth and defied the enemy with what equipment they had. The Germans scattered leaflets appealing to the troops to surrender after the disasters of Greece and Crete. Our troops' reply was to nail one of the leaflets to the mast in the main square of Tobruk and to put with it a banner marked, 'Come and get it'. That's the 'Tobruk Standard'.

But they needed more than courage and optimism. They've needed patience and plenty of it. For four months now they've been holding on without much activity. They've had to put up with heat, dust, salty water and not very varied food. They've done their share of grumbling at times, but they've even done their grumbling with a smile. They've never let discomforts or hardships get them down, they've only grown more keen to have a crack at the enemy which has made them fight in such Godforsaken country. But the waiting has tried their patience, especially in the salient. Conditions there have been anything but easy. Yet they've not only held their ground, they've forced the enemy back hundreds of yards and then dug themselves in again in new, improvised positions. To relieve the boredom of waiting, they've worked hard to make their positions better. Even during their spells in reserve, they've worked on new positions, drilling, blasting and digging their way through the unfriendly rock from early morning till dark, in heat and sandstorm. And by doing this they've made Tobruk infinitely stronger than it was when they came here.

Those are some of the elements of the 'Tobruk Standard' — courage, initiative, optimism, patience, ceaseless toil and, if necessary, complete sacrifice. This is the only standard which will win this war, and in it you won't find any room for complacency. You won't find it in Tobruk, because you can't live in a fortress with an enemy at your gate and still be complacent or still think that half-measures will do. We know that we will win only if everyone does all he can and gives all he can. I think from what I've said you'll realise that the Tobruk men have made a standard and they've kept to it. They've shown that they are worthy of the total backing of every Australian. The kind of backing they need is the backing of guns and tanks and planes and the backing of the money that will buy these things. Without that, the war is going to be more costly in human lives and longer in the winning. But if we get the equipment and the money that is urgently needed, we can go right on from here to victory.

Odd were the circumstances under which this broadcast (almost a world shortwave link-up) was made: just a 'mike' on a deal board table covered with an Army blanket, the truck carrying the necessary transmitting equipment hidden under a rocky escarpment some hundreds of yards away. It was hardly a BBC environment, but a setting suited to the spirit of those days.

Immediately I had concluded, the hardy technicians of the show, who had the matter in hand, invited me to their 'Army vehicle cum control room/ transmitting station' to hear a recording of my speech. To hear myself as others heard me was quite unlike what I expected, and I hope I didn't set the loan back any.

A patrol from the 2/13th
Battalion following a safety
tape through a mine field.
Tobruk. September 1941.
AWM 020782.

The youngest member of the
Polish Brigade at age fifteen,
Sanoica Zbigniew behind a
Bren gun. Tobruk, October, 1941.
AWM 020954.

Polish troops manning a heavy gun. Tobruk, October 1941. AWM 020977.

*A group of senior officers of the Polish Brigade,
Tobruk, April 1941. AWM 021051.*

Major General Morshead saying farewell to members of the Polish
Brigade. Tobruk, October 1941. AWM 021084.

Major General L. Morshead with high ranking Polish officers including
General Kopanski to his left. Tobruk, October 1941. AWM 021141.

Australian and Polish soldiers digging new positions for the Poles, Tobruk, September 1941. AWM 041841.

Jack Gambling and Corporal John Edmondson of 2/17th Battalion. Tobruk 1941. AWM P004426.003.

21

AUSSIES

(before Wo?)

AFTER CRETE DISASTER ANZAC TROOPS ARE NOW BEING RUTHLESSLY SACRIFICED BY ENGLAND IN TOBRUCH AND SYRIA.

TURKEY HAS CONCLUDED PACT OF FRIENDSHIP WITH GERMANY. ENGLAND WILL SHORTLY BE DRIVEN OUT OF THE MEDITERRANEAN. OFFENSIVE FROM EGYPT TO RELIEVE YOU TOTALLY SMASHED.

YOU CANNOT ESCAPE.

OUR DIVE BOMBERS ARE WAITING TO SINK YOUR TRANSPORTS. THINK OF YOUR FUTURE AND YOUR PEOPLE AT HOME.

COME FORWARD – SHOW WHITE FLAGS AND YOU WILL BE OUT OF DANGER !

SURRENDER !

Enemy propaganda leaflets dropped into Australian lines.

J. Smith of the 2/17th Battalion at the grave of Corporal John Edmondson VC. Tobruk. 1941. AWM P00426.005.

Corporal John Hurst (Jack) Edmondson VC, 2/17th
Battalion. Edmondson died on 14 April 1941 at Tobruk.
AWM P05150.001.

Chapter 7

Chapter 7

On occasions of minor activity, such as patrols to obtain enemy identification, it was usual for the CO concerned — and me — to take a couple of blankets each and spend the night in the front line, not out of any romantic thirst for danger, which is a thirst the desert quickly satisfies, but because desert nights are dark and desert headquarters are made modestly inconspicuous and would be difficult for the returning patrol commander to find. On one such night, Lieutenant Colonel Ogle and I, with some of our staffs, were waiting in an old Italian gun emplacement, a shallow, open pit known as 'the fishpond', and, to pass time, were taking turns singing songs. The name of my item escapes me and possibly escaped my audience too, as I have one of those voices that start well but have such a long, rough passage to travel that when they emerge there is some doubt about just what note they actually started on. Not so Lieutenant Colonel Ogle, who really can sing, and the returning patrol was no doubt cheered on its way by his tuneful rendering of Gounod's 'Ave Maria'.

Having received the patrol's report, I set out for home in Lieutenant Colonel Ogle's utility which picked its way in the darkness, often stopping so we could feel for the track with our feet. Between stopping and starting I chatted to the driver who, I discovered afterwards, was quite an identity and known affectionately to everyone as 'Old Jim'.

'I don't seem to have seen you about at all,' I remarked by way of making conversation.

'No, Sir, I been keepin' out o' yer way.'

'Why?' I asked.

'Well, Sir,' said Old Jim, 'they said as soon as yer saw me yer'd reckon I was too old.'

'What do you do with yourself then?'

'I've been pretty busy, Sir. They had me carrying dead and wounded out of the salient.'

'Well, son, if you're young enough for that, you're not too old for me.'

Jim talked of his life in Western Queensland until finally we reached my HQ safely, thanks mainly to his bushman's eyesight, and there Jim declined my offer to wait until daylight before going back to his battalion. 'They'll only be worrying about me,' were his last laconic words as he disappeared in the darkness.

Although among well-trained troops there is always an undercurrent of discipline and teamwork, in the course of a long siege there must also be a wealth of personal contacts and a store of humour contributed to by all ranks, including one Private Hattrick. This gentleman owed his last name to a story more often told than believed, concerning his former cricketing triumphs. At Tobruk, however, Private Hattrick's functions were of a rather more fundamental nature: in civil life he would have been called a nightman; in the Army he was variously and more picturesquely named, but I remember him for his association with the Iti wheelbarrow.

This wheelbarrow was a highly prized souvenir of Tobruk's former occupants and was, in fact, prized so highly that I had forbidden its use except with my permission or that of the Brigade Major, Bluey Allan. The thought of using that barrow in lieu of the traditional cart must have tempted Private Hattrick, as must the reflection that, as his duties were performed at the sleepy hour after stand-to, he was not likely to be detected. Finally one morning he succumbed to temptation, but he had reckoned without Bluey Allan, and his triumphant progress was suddenly checked by Bluey's stentorian shout: 'Hey! Put that thing away! You don't understand machinery!'

Private Hattrick was also the prototype of radar; he was our recognised air-raid warning, and the sight of our nightman running for cover was the usual signal for what he called 'rodents in the air'. However, like all human devices, Private Hattrick was not infallible; he was, in fact, just another child of nature and, one morning, nature called him suddenly to contribute to his own professional labours. Moreover, the call was apparently an imperious one, for he found it necessary to drop everything and run for what was locally known as 'the beehive'. This spectacle did not pass unnoticed and, naturally, it was misinterpreted, with the result that, on every hand, men began running for cover. Nor did the incident end there, for Private Hattrick, seeing the universal haste to be elsewhere, heard in it a call even more imperious than nature's, and himself joined in the mad rush with his task only half completed. I can appreciate his feeling because I also felt the urge to join in but, having watched the little play from beginning to end, I guessed that it all started with nature and not with 'rodents in the air', so I remained an amused spectator.

Some time later we lost our human warning device, as I found one day on a visit of inspection to rear echelon. Rear echelon is a collection of trucks and stores not actually needed in the line and, consequently, is to be found somewhere behind in the most attractive surrounding available. So it was here, but, as the desert has little to offer in the way of scenery, the greatest attraction was the sea, and inspections of rear echelon were more or less a professional excuse for a swim. I had had my swim when Private Hattrick appeared on the scene, and was in no mood to listen to the long and garbled story he insisted on telling, a fact which my driver, Hughie, remarked on as we drove back. 'It wasn't a bad story, just the same,' said Hughie. 'Apparently Hattrick wasn't feeling well, so evacuated himself to hospital, but after an air raid he no longer felt safe there, so evacuated himself to rear echelon. Now he feels that the only safety for him lies in the familiar surroundings of Brigade HQ and he wants you to un-evacuate him.'

Sometimes General Morshead would take a trip to GHQ in Cairo, a trip not without its perils, thanks to the attentive Stukas, and on these occasions I, the eternal 'glory boy', would delight in the fact that I was in sole command of the garrison of Tobruk. When one of these occasions found me at Divisional HQ, I decided to sleep under the stars rather than in the deserted building that was the Divisional Commander's home; I always did have kindly feelings for the stars, as I lived mostly with them. Accordingly, I had ordered taken outside my valise, that conglomeration of canvas, blankets, mosquito-netting and assorted old junk. Judge my surprise and envy when I saw nearby a magnificent structure complete with snowy white mosquito netting and looking for all the world like a bridal bed. I was even more surprised to find that the bridal bed belonged to one of the general staff officers, Colonel Charles Lloyd, and couldn't resist the gloomy reminder that 'You'll be sleeping in that alone, you know.'

When General Morshead returned, I talked to him so feelingly about the bright lights of Cairo that he promised me the next trip, for seven days.

'Seven days going, coming, or altogether?' I asked hopefully.

'Seven days the lot,' said the General, and thus was arranged my one brief escape from besieged Tobruk. I had my misgivings about this trip by the famous 'Tobruk Ferry Service' destroyers for, while I admired them, I found it difficult to share the nonchalance of our naval men. However, I reached the ship's side and, thanks to the efficiency of the Navy, safely cleared bomber point — that point where, if we had been observed, the Stukas would have been bound to pay us their undivided attention. It was sheer delight, too, to enter the wardroom which had been dedicated to us by the ship's officers who were too busy at action stations to occupy it, and to eat a meal of real bacon and eggs.

My thoughts on reaching Alexandria were of cold beer, the green of the Nile Delta and the cheerful sight of children playing, and I still had not become accustomed to the luxuries of civilisation when I eventually arrived in Cairo and went aboard one of the famous Nile houseboats. These craft had plied the river as far as Khartoum before the war, but were now converted to rest centres for officers returned from the desert. Kindly people on that boat used to ask me where I would go or what I would do and all I ever answered them was, 'I just want to lean over the rail and smoke cigarettes.' I could not even raise the enthusiasm to go shopping for family presents, so sent my batman, and he returned with prizes better than I could have bought and, he being a private soldier, infinitely cheaper. They included a black silk negligee with a silver dragon on the back, and I told my batman to try it on; he was of a suitable size and he pirouetted round the room in it asking me, who had been six months in Tobruk, how it looked. 'Too seductive,' I replied, 'take the damned thing off!'

That night, after a dozen baths, I arrayed myself in the best I had for a dance and a visit by General Sir Thomas Blamey, whom I had met briefly in this war but remembered best from the last, when he was Chief of Staff to

General Monash. In those days a school had been established near Amiens, thanks to General Blamey's farsightedness, to train officers in the tactics of open warfare after three years of confinement to the trenches. We infantry officers did not realise that we were mere pawns in the games of higher policy, sufficient for us that we liked that school because it gave us a spell out of the line. But after a visit and an address by General Blamey himself, we appreciated the wisdom of the higher policy, too.

But now it was Cairo and the Nile houseboat, a far cry from Amiens and that officers' school, and the General was paying a surprise visit. I was still a little overawed, quite unnecessarily as it proved, for we were all struck by his kindliness and the freedom of his manner; most great men, indeed, are gentle, for they have no need to bluster. The general asked me why he had not received a copy of the poem 'This Place They Call Tobruk', written by my driver, Hughie Paterson, in the style of his father, Banjo, copies of which had reached Cairo without my knowledge. I was having a souvenir made for General Blamey out of the base of a 25-pounder shell case, decorated with a 2-pound Iti mortar bomb, so I had a copy of the poem concealed in the tail fin of the bomb and duly presented. Long afterwards in Australia I told the General about this and there he found his presentation copy. With Hughie's permission I shall print the words of that poem here. We have been through so much together that this is no liberty.

This Place They Call Tobruk

By Hughie Paterson

There's places that I've been in
I didn't like too well,
New England's far too blooming cold
And Winton's hot as hell.
The Walgett beer is always warm,
In each there's something crook,
But each and all are perfect to
This place they call Tobruk.

We reckoned El Agheila
Was none too flash a place;
El Abier and Beda Fomm
Weren't in the bloody race.
At towns this side of Benghazi
We hadn't time to look,
But I'll take my oath they're better than
This place they call Tobruk.

I've seen some dust storms back at home
That made the housewives work,
Here there's enough inside our shirts
To smother all of Bourke.
Two diggers cleaned their dugout
And their blankets out they shook,
Two colonels perished in the dust in
This place they call Tobruk.

There's militant teetotallers
Who abhor all kinds of drink,
There's wives who break good bottles
And pour them down the sink.
This place would suit them to the ground,
We've searched in every nook,
But booze is rare as hen's teeth in
This place they call Tobruk.

There's centipedes like pythons
And there's countless hordes of fleas,
As big as poodle dogs they come
A-snapping round your knees.
And scorpions large as AFVs

Come out to have a look.[3]
There's surely lots of livestock in
This place they call Tobruk.

The shelling's nice and frequent
And they whistle overhead,
You go into your dugout
And find shrapnel in your bed.
And when the Stukas dive on us
We never pause to look,
We're down our holes like rabbits in
This place they call Tobruk.

Some times we go in swimming
And float about at ease,
The water clear as crystal
And a nice clean salty breeze.
When down comes blasted Hermann
And we have to sling our hook,
And we dive clean to the bottom in
This place they call Tobruk.

I really do not think this place
Was meant for me and you,
Let's return it to the Arab
And he knows what he can do.
We'll leave this God-forgotten place
Without one backward look,
We've called it lots of other names,
This place they call Tobruk.

---

3   AFVs: armoured fighting vehicles.

Having at last boiled the desert out of my person and feeling almost respectable again, the inclination came to me to see the sights of Cairo, including Kasr-el-nil Barracks, of which I had been adjutant for a period during the last war when a composite regiment was formed from Australian reinforcements to take charge pending the arrival of the British reliefs. It had appealed to my romantic nature, for Kasr-el-nil Barracks are historic; Napoleon once had his headquarters there and the mess still has the tall gilt mirrors of that French period. The balcony is said to have been added by Napoleon himself so that he could smoke his after-dinner cigar looking out over the Nile. I did not smoke cigars in those days, but we must all make sacrifices to romance and I thought the occasion warranted it. Years after, in one of my brief periods of leave, I was shaving in my own dressing-room and my young son asked me if I knew anything about Napoleon. 'Yes,' I replied, 'he was another great general,' and my baby of four saw in this no injustice to Napoleon, though the oddity did occur to me.

There was a sequel to my brief reign at Kasr-el-nil Barracks; two years later, in France, I received a bill printed on formal buff paper for the sum of £4.5.0, being the difference between the cost of four second-class and four third-class coffins. It had been one of my duties to arrange burial of British troops who died in hospital and, apparently, I had done four of them too well with second-class coffins, to which they were not entitled. I showed the bill to my then CO, who said there were only two things I could do: either frame it as a souvenir, or tear it up. I rather regret now that I adopted the easier course, and I hope this disclosure at so late a date will not involve Australia in diplomatic difficulties with the mother country.

And so, back to Tobruk by way of the 'Tobruk Ferry Service' from Alexandria, this time in the Australian destroyer *Stuart*, commanded by Captain Waller. I had heard that to be on Captain Waller's bridge was an experience to make one proud of being an Australian and, as he sat there in a home-knitted skull cap, there was no doubt on that bridge who was in command. His cabin was also at my disposal, his dressing table crowned with family photographs, his homely pipe rack and just the kind of books I liked; I felt almost that I was part of his family. But in spite of homely surroundings, we were still at war, as we realised soon after passing Matruh, when our signal-listening apparatus picked up a submarine. Our destroyer consort was diverted to cover the suspected area and, at the right moment, Captain Waller gave the order for five depth charges to be fired and then laconically ordered the ships back on their course, remarking to me in a voice he might have used at a tea party, 'If he's there, that'll fix him.'

In the inky blackness we stole into Tobruk harbour and at once unloading began, an embarrassment for my batman, Woolhouse, and myself for we had in our charge numerous parcels for the men of my HQ, such things as papers, peanuts and — must I confess it? — liquor. There was no standing on ceremony in those unloading operations, no rank or privileges, and I well remember how my stomach ached from the impact of packages thrown from the destroyer's deck down to me standing on the lighter. However, we got our contraband safely ashore and I slept out the night on bags of spuds and packing-cases, while my batman arranged transport. This arrived at dawn, and so I returned to my HQ in a blaze of glory, having successfully carried out every request.

War brings a wealth of heroism, some of it that unspectacular kind for which no citation or award is possible and, looking back on it now, an example of this appeals to me — the quiet heroism of Archie Lee.

Archie was our sergeant of transport who, some time previously, had been medically boarded for a suspected cancer of the throat and was due to be evacuated. Now he had himself paraded to me to ask if he might remain. 'I know I'm going to die, Sir,' he said, 'but why can't it be here with all of you?'

'Well, Lee,' I replied, 'the decision is yours,' and, taking his papers from among the files on my table, I tore them up and threw them in the basket. All I could say as I shook hands was, 'Well, here we go.'

But it couldn't go on like that indefinitely and Archie became so weak that eventually he did have to be evacuated, and I saw him next a year later in an Australian General Hospital near Sydney, where Mrs Murray and I paid him a visit. By this time Archie's voice was only a husky whisper, but his courage was still on top, and what he wanted to talk about was the humour and the jokes of Tobruk. However, miracles still happen — there was no cancer and, after a successful operation, Archie recovered. I met him again during the 'flap' of Japan's entry into the war, when I was responsible for the defence of one of our cities, the city where Archie worked. He had not forgotten us; every day there were flowers for Mrs Murray at her hotel and when I was too fully occupied with my military duties, Archie was always her willing escort. Memory ceases an hour after we cease and, until that time, I will remember the quiet soldier who could withstand the desert, a siege and illness, all at once.

Unloading stores from a transport ship in Tobruk Harbour,
April 1941. AWM 007501.

Dust from a German bomb, but little damage. Tobruk,
August 1941. AWM 009530.

Constructing a rail line through a tunnel. Tobruk, September 1941. AWM 020200.

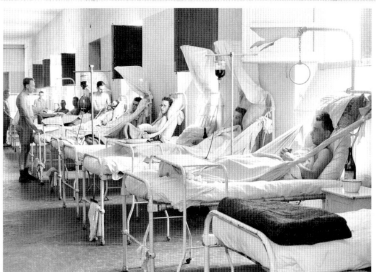

Patients in the main ward in the surgical section of the 4th Australian General Hospital. Tobruk, September 1941. AWM 020323.

Soldier shaving at a
dugout in a forward area.
Tobruk. September 1941.
AWM 020494.

Leisure time at Tobruk,
swimming, fishing and
writing home. September 1941.
AWM 020620.

Libyan desert around Tobruk with a burning enemy plane in the distance. 1941. AWM 040613.

B Company of 2/13th Battalion during a truce to allow the Germans to recover their dead after a battle the previous evening. Tobruk, May 1941. AWM 128992.

Brigadier J. J. Murray
on leave in Egypt, 1941.
Murray family collection.

The HMAS Stuart commanded by Captain Waller took Brigadier
J. J. Murray to Egypt for leave. AWM P00444.186.

Captain Waller led the 'Scrap Iron Flotilla' of five aged Australian
destroyers, which sustained the garrison during the Siege of Tobruk. He
later captained HMAS Perth and went down with his ship off Java in 1942.

Chapter 8

Chapter 8

After my epoch-making week in Alexandria and Cairo, life had to settle down again somehow to a state of siege with all the loneliness that involved, and which could not always be concealed. I liked to think it was sometimes for companionship, as well as for military reasons, that General Morshead would seek me out, because there is more loneliness at the top than anywhere else, and his theme song might have been, 'In My Solitude'. So it was that when, one morning after my return, the General came over, ostensibly to discuss that already worn-out subject, our plan of defence, I suggested a tour of Battalion HQ with the deliberate intention of getting him away from himself and regaling him with stories of home and things nearer the heart than the head.

As we bumped across the desert, I was reminded of an incident long ago, though it concerned the tarmac roads of civilisation and not a stony desert, when I was driving my family; Mrs Murray was sitting beside me and giving me one of those ear-thumpings from which I am still a little deaf on the left side, this time about the frailties of husbands generally and of this husband in particular. Some of the effect was lost, however, when my eight-year-old daughter piped up from the back seat, 'Mummy, Daddy's wicked but he's interesting.'

Not only generals and brigadiers have wives and worries. One soldier wrote home along these lines: 'My dear wife, you always did nag me when I was at home and now you keep writing long, nagging letters. Why can't you be quiet and let me enjoy the war in peace?'

General Morshead said he never had so many laughs to the square yard of desert before, and one story he particularly liked concerned my son, Peter, then aged seven, and a couple of dozen oysters, which I had brought home for supper for my wife and me. For reasons best known to himself, Peter was sleepless that night and, during supper, he appeared in pyjamas and slippers and sat in on the oysters, which he had never seen before. My wife put two on his plate and then our attention returned to our own oysters and ourselves and Peter was forgotten. When my wife and I looked up again, Peter's face was working and there was a strained expression on it. 'What's the matter, Peter?' she asked, 'Don't you want any more oysters?' 'No thanks,' came the muffled reply. 'I don't even want this one!' We extricated Peter from his difficulties by removing the offending oyster.

There was need for humour as relief from the other emotions. At about this time, those of us who could leave our duties for the moment — and there were not very many of us, because large assemblies were not possible under enemy eyes — attended the dedication of a monument to our fallen. It was a fine monument, built by our engineers of concrete and such other stores as were available in our dumps, and erected in the one cemetery of Tobruk where British, Australians, Indians and Poles lay in their rough soldiers' graves, a fine monument of Empire. The ceremony brought back to my mind a thought never far away, of how, if spared, I was to explain these graves to the families of the fallen and see in their eyes the unspoken question, 'Why should they have been taken and you left?' I had experienced this after the last war and still cannot meet on equal terms the people of my men who were lost. My feelings are best expressed by the inscription on that monument:

'At the going down of the sun and in the morning we shall remember them.'

Some days after the dedication, General Morshead and I returned to the cemetery and walked around among the graves which were being decorated and cared for by thoughtful friends. All manner of soldiers were there and they talked and smoked at their work, but something about them struck me and I asked General Morshead, 'Have you noticed anything unusual about the men?'

'No, everything seems much as usual.'

'Have you noticed that in half an hour you have not heard one soldier swear?'

'Well, John, now that you mention it, neither I have.'

These men would have resented it had they been accused of sentiment, but they had their own way of showing their respect, and not one of those graves was left unattended.

We had now to take over that portion of the line known as the salient, a hastily constructed line of defences marking the limit of the German penetration of our perimeter in May. Owing to the proximity of the Germans and the fact that they overlooked our makeshift positions, the holding of this area was no sinecure. I was anxious to get identification of the German units opposing us, and instructed a battalion to send patrols out for the purpose, giving orders that I was to be woken as soon as any information was to hand. This was done, but the corporal who came back from the patrol to give it to me was too tired to think of anything except that it had been successful. All I could get out of him was that he had found a couple of Itis in a hole, one asleep and the other drowsy; that he had wakened them both with the bayonet and, after that, there had been no further trouble. There was no mention of where this hole was, the distance and compass bearing, any papers, or anything else that might identify the Italian unit. All the corporal cared was that he had done his job and wanted sleep. Naturally, my curiosity was not satisfied and, for a while, the wires buzzed until I had a more complete report of the night's work.

My HQ was in a rocky gully on the side of which, farthest from the enemy, we had some old Italian 75-mm field guns which drew a good deal of enemy shellfire. As my HQ collected its share of the hot shell fragments as well as all the drop-shorts, things were sometimes rather intense, and we hugged what cover there was. My erstwhile batman, Murray, thinking of our safety and, no doubt, his own as well, suggested moving farther up the gully, but as that was no better than where we were, I declined. However, I told Murray he could go there himself if he liked. So off went Murray on a reconnaissance and, by some strange chance, he had just arrived at what was to be his 'better 'ole' when the enemy began to shell it, and we were treated to the spectacle of Murray leaping from rock to rock in his haste to return to us, his thirst for exploration well satisfied.

Murray still had his bright ideas, though, and one was to enlarge Bluey Allan's dugout in the side of the gully. Here he dug with the pick for hours into chalky rock, but progress was too slow and, having once been a miner in the course of a varied career, he decided to blow it out with gelignite. Progress was rapid enough then, even for Murray's taste, and too much so for Bluey, who called me from my office-cum-bedroom dugout nearby to come and view the remains. What had once been a dugout was now an open fissure in the rock; and what had been its roof was nothing but a heap of rubble hopelessly mingled with the remnants of Bluey's personal effects.

At about this time, the Itis were erecting two prefabricated iron towers opposite our lines, and it was obvious to all the world that their purpose was to give observation over our positions. However, a young subaltern paying a visit to HQ from his battalion, hard put to it for some topic to open a conversation with me, chose those towers and solemnly asked, 'What do you think they are for, Sir?' I had a mind to read him a lesson on the matter of frivolous questions, so I just as solemnly replied, 'Well, I have it on the best authority that they are to be the new Iti broadcasting station, but so far the Itis have only two gramophone records: 'Come over here' and 'I can't give you anything but love, baby'. The subaltern retired rather disconsolately and, no doubt, with ideas of his own about flippancy in high places.

Even in places like the salient, familiarity with danger is apt to breed contempt, but we could generally rely on a little diversion whenever we ventured out of it, as Bluey Allan found one day when he drove out with two officers in a utility to bring in some machine-guns from our left flank. This time the source of interest was our own tactical minefields, so prodigally sewn round our positions that movement among them, even by us, had to be cautious. Blue negotiated them safely this time and, having picked up a heavy load of machine-guns, the rest seemed easy, for he had only to come back to safety along his own tracks. So thought Blue and, no doubt, he felt considerably aggrieved (among other things) when a mine exploded under the added weight of the load and blew the back of the truck off. Blue came to me with a 'touch of the Joe Blakes' and no machine-guns. I found a drop of strong rum to cure the shakes, but nothing could alter his conviction that there should have been no mine and that fate had played him a dirty trick.

At that time, we still had elements of the famous British Machine Gun Regiment, the Royal Northumberland Fusiliers, giving support on various parts of our front. One day, as I was driving round our positions, I saw a soldier, obviously British, lowering his water bottle by the cord into one of the infrequent desert wells. The sight made me immediately thirsty, so I drove over and asked for a drink, which he courteously gave me. By way of making conversation, I asked, 'What do you belong to?'

'The NFs, Sir.'

'Where are your gun positions, hereabouts?' I pursued conversationally.

'If I knew who you were,' he answered, his caution not the least affected by the brass hat I was wearing, 'I'd tell you that, too.'

I had imagined that everyone in my command knew me, but apparently I meant nothing in his young life — he had his orders and meant to carry them out.

Our next move took me back to a former HQ of mine, nearby which was a huge cave or cistern, dug out of rock. I have never found a satisfactory explanation for these cisterns so often found in the desert, perhaps the Bedouin used them to store grain or water; but this one had evidently been used by the Italians as a church to judge from the remnants of an altar and a cross roughly marked in charcoal on the wall above it. Now, however, it was to provide the stage and an auditorium for the one and only Tobruk concert.

Here I must attempt to describe the indescribable. There was to be a one-act play and, in addition, there were individual contributions from such artists as a violinist from the Royal Horse Artillery and his pet white rat, which crawled all over him and his instrument as he played, and a tall Queenslander whose recitations took me back to a drovers' camp in faraway Australia. Another noteworthy performer was a descendant from the original Australians who sang, or rather monologued, such pieces as 'Why Should I Work When I Can Sing?' — I made a mental note that he would probably have to work after all — and a rambling history of Ned Kelly, all out of time with the music. His unorthodox performance nearly brought the cave in on us.

The Divisional Commander and some of his staff were our guests at the concert, and in his few words of appreciation to the artists — and what artists! — he remarked that if we survived we might see many concerts the world over, but none that would live in our memories like this one. He also said in an aside to me during the performance, 'It's a bit hot, John, isn't it?'

'You should have seen it last night,' I replied, 'I've censored it since!'

It was also broadcast, or rather, such parts of it as were considered suitable for those who were either too young or too old to appreciate the rest.

The *piéce de resistance* was, of course, the one-act play, and here I must choose my words carefully. It concerned a Mr and Mrs Barren who, as the name implies, were childless. The government of the mythical country where they lived had decreed that all married couples must have children, in default of which a government agent would be provided to supply any natural deficiencies. The curtain went up on a stage furnished mostly with packing cases and lit by smoking oil lamps, and disclosed a gentleman dressed in morning coat and bowler hat — procured from heaven knows what obscure Italian source — and below these gorgeous articles, just plain issue trousers and dusty boots. This was Mr Barren, who was preparing to depart when a caller arrived in the person of a travelling photographer who specialised in babies and wished to photograph Mr Barren's children. This was naturally a sore point with Mr Barren in view of the government decree, and the photographer departed rather abruptly, followed closely by Mr Barren.

Next to appear was Mrs Barren, nervously rearranging non-existent ornaments in the sitting room and obviously a prey to apprehension, not of the audience or the play, but of the impending visit by the government agent. She was dressed in red silk over an ample figure, which was obviously upholstered with respirators and such like wherever they were needed most. To her came a gentleman attired in civilian suit and felt hat, with pince-nez and a portfolio of papers, and was received by Mrs Barren with a coyness suggestive of abandon; in fact, it took him some time to extricate himself and explain that he was not the expected agent, but only a clerk in that department whose job it was to make the proceedings valid. Mrs Barren registered disappointment, but let it go at that.

The next visitor was the photographer again, taking the opportunity to interview Mrs Barren in her husband's absence. He was, of course, mistaken for the much-anticipated agent and received even more seductively than the clerk. However, before getting down to business, he persuaded her to see some samples of his art, in the form of countless photographs of all sorts and sizes of babies. Mrs Barren evinced some concern over a pair of twins which the photographer assured her he had got in a shop window, but at the sight of triplets obtained on the top of a double-decker bus, she swooned away and the curtain fell on Tobruk's one-act play. At the moment of writing, Mrs Barren is a captain fighting in Borneo. I have often twitted him since about that part and he told me, 'I'll never live that down with you, Sir, will I?'

Returning from these flights of fancy, I found that the war was still going on. Being a moonlit night there was the usual air raid and, after that, a phone call from Divisional HQ saying that a bit of offensive action was to be carried out on another sector and I was to make a demonstration in the morning to deceive the enemy. It was all rather insolent conduct for a besieged garrison, but I said I would do what I could. At daylight I took some of my officers in the only two staff cars available and sent a message to Lieutenant Colonel Crawford, in command of the El Adem sector, to meet us there in his. We then drove down the El Adem Road and drew up against our wire, got out of our cars and walked up and down the wire, alternately peering through our binoculars and talking earnestly to little groups of men as though issuing orders. After a quarter of an hour of this, I felt we had done enough and that, having drawn the crabs, it would be a good idea to get clear before the enemy shelling started. Just as we were leaving, I saw a young artillery subaltern perched on an observation tower watching our clowning with interest, not unmixed with apprehension. 'Would you mind telling me what it's all about, Sir?' he called down. 'Oh,' I replied, 'we were just drawing Jerry's attention so that he'll think there's an attack going over here, and now we're getting out before he does anything about it.' 'That's alright for you, Sir,' the subaltern answered, 'but I've got to stay!' I thought of him when I heard the shells coming over a little later as we drove home. I did not neglect to make enquiries and found that no-one suffered anything worse than temporary discomfort — mental discomfort in that subaltern's case, as he had remained in his tower while the others went to ground.

Our complete isolation from the rest of the world set a premium on pets of all sorts. There was, for instance, Crawford's cat, which was highly valued by its owner but less highly by me, owing to the animal's playful habit of perching up among the stones of Lieutenant Colonel Crawford's HQ and leaping down onto my bare knees with all its claws extended. Crawford went to no end of trouble to circumvent this, but sooner or later, when our attention was distracted, the animal always managed to get in one jump. Then there was Ogle's monkey, which would sit on its master's shoulder while he went his rounds of the positions and, at other times, used to be tied up to a truck by a light chain. There it was, an endless source of amusement, jumping about all over the truck, but always ending these antics at the first sign of an air raid, to dive chattering for cover under the engine. Our amusement over this performance was some consolation for the discomfort of the raids.

But, pets or no pets, the siege went on. The Italians had two long-range guns which were causing a good deal of annoyance, and we decided to send out a patrol to spike them. I will not worry the reader with details but, briefly, it was to be a large patrol, four officers and forty men in all, who were to pass through a gap prepared in the enemy minefields, penetrate his lines, and then follow a road we knew of until it brought them to the spot where we had located the guns. Those were the days before rubber-soled desert boots, and we had only the ordinary military boots, which make a great deal of noise on stony ground. So, on reaching the road, the patrol sat down and removed its boots as pre-arranged, not a word being spoken. On they went then in their stockinged feet, as far as the position where the guns should have been and farther; but alas, those precious guns were withdrawn when not actually firing, so there was nothing left for the patrol to do but return, put on their boots again, then back through the enemy lines and minefields, and so home to bed. One man, however, could not find his boots, so an officer gave him his own pair and they moved off again. Soon they were sufficiently clear of the enemy lines to be able to check their numbers, and this time it was a man that couldn't be found, so the stocking-footed officer set back to look for him. He found him at last, still sitting where the patrol had removed its boots, blissfully unaware that he had been left behind, such was the silence of a patrol's movements. By the time those two got back the officer's feet were cut about and his socks soaked with blood, and all to no purpose. This gives some indication of what patrolling meant, and there were nightly occurrences such as this.

War cemetery on the Bardia – Tobruk Road, Tobruk, April 1941. AWM 007562.

Major General Morshead addresses troops from the steps of the memorial to the heroes of Tobruk. October 1941. AWM 010320.

Operations room of the 9th Australian Division Signals.
Tobruk, 1941. AWM 020296.

Major General L. J. Morshead and Brigadier J. J. Murray leaving
advanced Headquarters, 9th Division. Tobruk August 1941. AWM 020303.

The observation post
of the 107th Regiment,
Royal Horse Artillery.
Tobruk, August 1941.
AWM 020384.

A patrol from the 2/13th Battalion travelling over
open ground. Tobruk, September 1941. AWM 020783.

Solider from the 2/17th
Battalion being carried
into the 'fig tree'
regimental aid post.
Tobruk, September 1941.

Soldiers at the wire. Tobruk, 1941. Author's photograph.

Lieutenant Colonel R. W. Ogle
(2/15th) with 'Ogle's monkey',
the Battalion mascot. Tobruk,
1941.
Author's photograph.

Brigadier R. W. Tovell,
26th Brigade, reading in
his dugout. Tobruk, 1941.
AWM P02242.007.

Chapter 9

Chapter 9

Siege or no siege, the British national game of cricket was not neglected. On a deserted aerodrome to the rear of our lines, games would be played between the various units whenever their men could be spared. It was here that the Tobruk Test was played out in a fashion reminiscent of hundreds of such tests in the past and, like them, played between an all-English and an all-Australian side, but having a few peculiarities of its own as well. To provide for these peculiarities, an operation order, which is given below, was published, and a poem by Hughie Paterson commemorates the occasion.

Cricket Match

Between

20 Aust Inf Bde HO. and 107 R.H.A.

To be played at Tobruk Cricket Ground.

1. Time of Start: Play to commence at 1400 hours 30 July, 1941.

2. Hours of Play: Play to be continuous, except for interference of air raids, until 1800 hours; play will not repeated not cease during shellfire.

3. Refreshments: All players will supply own beer. [Note: there was none.] Rum issue, before and after match, is being arranged by manager. [Note: the manager failed to perform this miracle.]

4. Dress: Shirt, shorts, long socks, sandshoes (if available), hats F.S. (or bareheaded), Iti helmets or other fancy headgear will not be worn. Umpires will wear white coat (if available) and will carry loaded rifle with fixed bayonet. Tin hats to be used (on heads only) by wicketkeepers, if desired.

5. <u>Umpires</u>: One umpire to be supplied by each side. Unbiased umpires preferred, but these may be changed if things are going against team concerned. Remarks to umpires on receipt of adverse decisions to be confined to those words used during dive-bombing attacks.

6. <u>Weapons</u>: All players will be searched for concealed weapons before start of play; all weapons found, other than S.T. grenades, Mills bombs, and revolvers will be confiscated. This does not apply to umpires.

7. <u>Additional Rules</u>; Any other rules may be added or deleted, as a majority of players, umpires or onlookers think fit.

8. <u>Medical</u>: Manager will make medical arrangements and have ambulance in attendance.

Signed: G.I. Worry Brig.

TOBRUK TEST
By Hughie Paterson

You've heard of Bradman, Hammond,

McCartney, Woodful, Hobbs,

You've heard of how McDougal topped the score,

Now I'd like to tell you how we play cricket in Tobruk,

In a way the game was never played before.

The players are a mixture,

They come from every rank,

And their dress would not be quite the thing at Lords,

But you don't need caps and flannels and expensive batting gloves,

To get the fullest sport the game affords.

The wicket's rather tricky,

For it's mat on desert sand,

But for us it's really plenty good enough,

And what with big bomb craters and holes from 9-inch shells,

The outfield could be well described as rough.

The boundary's partly tank trap,
With the balance Dannert wire,
And the grandstand's just a bit of sandy bank,
While our single sightboard's furnished by a shot down Jerry plane
And the scorer's in a ruined Iti tank.

One drawback is a minefield,
Which is at the desert end,
And critics might find fault with this and that,
But to us all runs are good ones even if a man should score
Four leg byes off the top of his tin hat.

The barracking is very choice,
The Hill would learn a lot,
If they could listen in to all the cries,
As the quartermaster sergeant bowls the Colonel neck and crop,
With a yorker, while some dust is in his eyes.

And the time the signal's runner
Scored the winning hit,
When, as he sprinted round the wire to try and save the four
The Battery Sergeant Major fell into a crater deep,
And the batsmen ran another seven more.

If we drive into the minefield,
We always run it out
For that is what our local rule defines,
It's always good for six at least, sometimes as high as ten,
While the fieldsman picks his way in through the mines.

Though we never stop for shellfire,
We're not too keen on planes,
But when the Stukas start to hover round,

You can sometimes get a wicket if you're game enough to stay
By bowling as the batsmen go to ground.

So, when we're back in Sydney,
And others start to talk
Of cricket, why we'll quell them with a look,
'You blokes have never seen a game of cricket properly played
The way we used to play it at Tobruk.'

It would have required a visionary's imagination to have seen in these players with their assorted Army clothing the flannelled and be-capped cricketers of our peaceful days. But nonetheless, it did recall memories of hours spent sitting in the bleachers, and it aroused hopes that such times would return.

We were always aware that our security depended on offensive action rather than on waiting passively for the enemy to probe us out, and many and varied were the schemes cooked up by officer and private alike to show our friends across the wire that we were on our toes. Once, for example, we roneod off onto large sheets of paper a bold 'V' with under it the inscription 'V for Victory', and we sent these out with every patrol to be pinned on enemy wire and minefields and any other conspicuous place that could be found. Unfortunately, we do not know what result followed, or what the enemy's reaction was to this campaign, but it was only one of dozens.

Constant alertness was the watchword of the garrison and, throughout the hours of darkness, our wire and our anti-tank ditch were always patrolled, despite the fact that beyond these we would have numerous fighting and reconnaissance patrols. Thus originated what came to be called the 'love and kisses patrol'.

Two men would be responsible for two adjoining sectors of the wire and it was necessary for each to know that all was well in the other's sector. To do this, the normal procedure was for them to wait for each other periodically at the junction of their sectors but, of course, this involved delay and waiting, so something better was introduced. Each was given a baton, one inscribed 'love', and the other 'kisses'. When love arrived at the junction point, he put his baton on the ground, and kisses, on his arrival, placed his on top of it.

Then when love returned he took his from underneath and placed it on top and so, in turn, did kisses. Thus the game went on and each knew that since his last visit the other had been there and that all was well with him. It was simplicity itself and, no doubt, not nearly as interesting to the participants as the original time-honoured game of that name; but such little frivolities all help to keep spirits high, and it was, after all, high spirits that held Tobruk.

Often at night we would carry out a tour of inspection of our forward positions along one sector or another. This was always a tricky business for the inspecting visitor because of the mines and wires and booby-traps laid so ingeniously for the foot of the unwary, and known fully only to the local occupants of those palatial holes in the ground which were our forward positions. It was poor consolation to know that one false step would mean promotion for all the others.

On one of these forays, Hughie drove me to the sector commander's post and left me there to continue the inspection on foot while he drove back and then around in a wide circuit to pick me up again at the other end of the sector. This time I had bitten off rather more than I really wanted to chew and, what with winding tortuously in and out of minefields and being handed over from one guide to another, practically the whole night was taken up while I thought enviously of Hughie sitting comfortably in the car and perhaps a cup of hot coffee waiting at the end of the road. I must have voiced some of my impatience, but the sector commander had his answer pat: 'I always did want to be a brigadier, Sir, and if you take one step I don't tell you to, there'd be a vacancy.' I carried on in chastened silence.

However, the inspection finally ended with our arrival at the last post, where I found Hughie sitting in the post itself with its defenders, and learnt from him afterwards as we drove home the effect my approach had had on them. The bush telegraph had been working overtime; each post in turn was forewarned of my coming, and in the last one they had taken the extreme precaution of doubling the sentries. This, as it proved, was nearly a fatal mistake, for each sentry tried to leave to the other the privilege of challenging me, and quite a hot, though whispered argument developed before one of them finally took the plunge, the challenge was made and answered, and I was admitted to the post.

On hearing this, my mind went back to the days of the last war when we had a similar bush telegraph. I was then acting Battalion Commander in my Colonel's absence, and I had my private arrangements with the Divisional HQ that some junior officer would ring me up and say the lance corporal was coming whenever the General, Sir Talbot Hobbes, planned a surprise visit. On this occasion orders had been given that each pillbox was to be rationed and munitioned for a siege in case it was cut off by penetration of our line, and picks, shovels and bombs were to be on hand so that, if necessary, we could dig or fight our way out. There was nothing wrong with the window display in my post —rations and ammunition were there, picks and shovels conspicuously present, and set into the concrete wall was a large box boldly marked in white paint 'bombs'. True, there was nothing at the moment in that box more lethal than scotch whisky, but what need to worry when we had our bush telegraph system? We were not worrying — in fact we chose that morning to pour ourselves a drink. But even the best schemes fail, as our telegraph failed that morning, and so it was that we were placidly sipping scotch and soda when in walked the General, unannounced, to see how his orders were being carried out. His eyes took in the picks and shovels, the rations and ammunition, but they were held by the bold lettering on that bomb box, and he strode over to lift the lid while all eyes followed him. But even generals have their weaknesses and Sir Talbot Hobbes' weakness was signalling. Moreover, our signal officer was well aware of this and, at the eleventh hour, he called to us from outside where he had been playing about with a Lucas signalling lamp, 'I've got communication with Brigade HQ at last, Sir. Would you care to come and see?' The General cared, the situation was relieved and, with one concerted rush of officers and batmen, the incriminating whisky was changed to bombs and the box became once again true to label.

One of the soldiers with the rather morbid habit of visiting and crawling all over the sunken wrecks in Tobruk harbour in his spare time, was goggle-eyed to find, staring up at him from the hold of one of them, the delectable label 'McEwen's Ale', with only fifteen feet of clear Mediterranean standing between him and his thirst. It was not long before I received a delicate approach from some of my braves for permission to organise a diving party. The catch in this was that, of course, anything salved would be the property of the whole garrison, and this rather cooled their ardour. I was sympathetic, but forgot all about the incident until some days later, when I received a further request and gave consent. Unfortunately for our diving party, the fuel oil bunkers of this particular wreck had sprung a leak and the once clear Mediterranean water had become rather a mess, but nothing like the mess our thirsty divers became. Having ventured so far they decided to proceed, and the game was on! It was a chastened party that returned to our lines, and they must have been days removing the oily stains of their adventures with the meagre supply of water available. No doubt, from the dusky recesses of that hold, the McEwen's Ale label still smiles temptingly up in that now-forgotten harbour.

It is rather a shock at times to find one's belief that, in that close-walled garrison one must be known to everybody, rudely shattered, but even more shattering was my experience of being taken for a fifth columnist. Climbing one day up an artillery observation tower with one of the divisional staff, then Major White, I asked all sorts of pertinent questions of the young British artillery officer there, but it was not till later I learned the explanation for his evasive answers. After I left him, he had phoned through to my HQ and reported 'A strange brigadier up here asking all sorts of questions with an officer he calls "White". Is he all right?' These fresh-faced, young English subalterns had a way of acquainting me with my own unimportance.

The incident took me back to the far-off days of the Somme Battle in the last war. The Germans had withdrawn voluntarily from a salient to shorten their line and thus save many troops. We received a communiqué ('comic cuts' to the very young) to the effect that the enemy had left in the abandoned area some of their own troops in our uniforms —spies, of course. One Clyne, a humble soldier who always felt that the whole weight of the European war was on his shoulders, and to whom the carrying out of instructions was always a personal matter of the gravest importance, listened attentively to the communiqué. Things were quiet now, and Clyne took his rifle and went out to see if he could shoot a hare or two in a nearby copse. He presented a strange sight as he crawled stealthily from tree to tree, rifle in hand — his hair had been without the attentions of a barber for months and his uniform was battle-stained. Some of our artillery witnessed his performance and were duly impressed; unfortunately for Clyne, they also had that communiqué in mind, so they promptly arrested him. At Battalion

HQ we received a phone call informing us that a man wearing our uniform had been detained. As he seemed unable to give a clear account of himself, would we send someone over to identify him? The CO said to me, 'Murray, you'd better fork your horse and ride over.' On arrival in the artillery lines, I found Clyne surrounded by seven of our gunners who, apparently, had been putting him through the third degree. At the sight of my familiar countenance he looked up and said, 'It's all right, Major, I haven't told 'em a bloody word.' This was loyalty the Germans could never have coped with, even if it was misdirected.

Great preparations at this time were being made by our own people for a big push from the direction of Alexandria and the Egyptian frontier. Secretly, in the dead of night, tanks were to arrive in Tobruk to strengthen the garrison for their task of supporting this push and positions for the concealment of these tanks had to be plotted, and holes dug to protect them from bombing. In one of my brief periods in command of the garrison, I heard that a considerable quantity of rum had accumulated and I approved of an issue or two. Shortly after one of these rare and auspicious occasions, a soldier, hammering with his pick to dig out a hole for one of the expected tanks, was heard to say, 'I've a lot of time for that bastard Murray.' Such is fame!

Now rumours were flying in all directions: relief was in the air and not all our security precautions could stop the news spreading. There came to us one day, to take charge of these tanks, one Brigadier Willesdon, a British tank commander, thin and red-headed, his sparse frame exuding energy. A much decorated veteran of the last war, he was a sheer delight to me to reminisce with over old battles, and I still smile over his description of a course he attended at one of Britain's most famous staff colleges. At the end of the course, the late General Sir John Dill, the Commandant of the school at the time, sent for 'the ant', as Brigadier Willesdon was familiarly styled (in a way he did resemble an ant — one of the soldier variety). Said General Dill, 'I suppose, Willesdon, you would like to know what manner of report I have made to the War Office on you?' 'The ant' agreed that he would. 'Well, I have reported that there is no man I would sooner have with me in a tight corner than you' (at this stage the ant would throw out his chest) 'and, Willesdon,' continued the General, 'I have also told them there is no-one I know would get me into a tight corner quicker.'

Still the rumours flew. There began to trickle in elements of a British division, the forerunners of their advance parties. Little Tich, the barber, neglected to ask the time-honoured question, 'Cut or trim, Sir?' and, taking the answer for granted, concentrated on trimming. The question now was who would be first out. We were to be the last, though at that time we did not realise what this was going to mean, and what a long, long last it was going to be. Brigadier Arthur Godfrey's brigade was to be relieved first and I was to take over his reinforcements and such of his personal effects as I could cajole him into leaving; no difficult task this, as he could take only what he could carry on his back. The men, too, participated in this then unknown lease-lend; the outgoers, with thoughts of cool beer and green fields ahead, were much more generous than normally in disgorging long-treasured possessions, and we who remained fell heirs to such things as a cracked cup or two, battered primus stoves and smelly pillows.

Here I must introduce Private Hattrick again, for he was indirectly responsible for our inheritance of the best chattel Arthur Godfrey bestowed. I had occupied my new HQ before, but could not find the old familiar place that stands alone and, on asking Private Hattrick, he pointed out to me the new site. I never could cope with his insatiable architectural ambitions, so accepted this latest creation philosophically, and it was only some days later I learned the grim realities behind this change of site for our house of evacuation. Hattrick, with his customary wariness of anything explosive, had turned down the old site because it was completely taken up by boxes of bombs, but this did not explain why, just at this time, we suddenly began to have lots of tinned fruit with our meals. However, my batman did. 'You see, Sir,' he told me with a grin, 'Hattrick turned down the old site but, on souveniring the bomb boxes, he found they were full of tinned fruit' — Arthur Godfrey's best legacy.

Brigadier Ray Tovell was next to go, and I paid him a farewell visit. A most amusing apparition met my eye, arranged in field service uniform of real cloth — so unlike the shirt and shorts that had served him so many months as morning dress, day dress, evening wear and even pyjamas. 'Ray!' I exclaimed, 'You look gorgeous. I could kiss you,' and I did. This was too much for General Kopanski, our Polish general, who could not bear to be left out of it. Thinking, apparently, that we shared his national custom, he joined in with a will and kissed each of us on both cheeks. Ray actually blushed, and maybe I did, too.

We were now a small minority, most of our line being taken over by a famous British division, and my fellows looked anxiously towards me to know why they had been left. Without any desire to overtax the patience of my readers (if any), I will repeat here an order of the day which, in part, satisfied the appetite of those gluttons for honour.

Order of the Day

by

Brigadier J.J. Murray, DSO, MC, VD

Commanding 20th Australian Infantry Brigade, AIF

Tobruk, 20th October, 1941.

We have the honour to be the last brigade to leave Tobruk. It is a tribute to your efficiency. Each of you has given to the defence of this fortress the full extent of your skill, courage and endurance, without which it would have been impossible to hold it. A very high standard has been set and we must keep that standard.

In the days that lie ahead you may be assured that every effort will be made to ensure for you a well-earned rest, with the fullest possible amenities. It is confidently expected that on the journey out to our destination the brigade will move with the perfect discipline that has characterised our previous operations.

Before coming to Libya we were a brigade under training untried, but we now have a tradition to preserve. Many of our men died to make this tradition and they remain in Tobruk. Remember them, for their honour and your own is in the keeping of every single soldier of the brigade.

Brigadier.

The 'V' for Victory sign.
These were left behind
enemy lines by night patrols
of the 20th Brigade. Tobruk,
August 1941. AWM 009394.

Wounded soldier being carried
into an underground aid post
in an advanced area. Tobruk,
September 1941. AWM 021020.

Matilda II infantry tanks of the 7th Battalion, Royal Tank Regiment moving across desert sand, Tobruk, September 1941. AWM 021039.

Crater caused when an enemy plane dropped a sea mine on the waterfront, Tobruk, October 1941. AWM 021074.

*Using a captured Italian anti-aircraft gun to ward of
German planes. Tobruk, 1941. AWM 040607.*

*Soldiers occupying front line positions against the
Italian front line. Tobruk, August 1941. AWM 041790.*

Soldiers crossing the Somme River near Peronne during the First World War. AWM A03511.

Western Front: First of our men to cross the Somme, near Peronne

Reinforcements of the 1st Division, AIF, on the Somme River in France in December 1916. AWM E00037.

Brigadier J. J. Murray's 'Tobruk
Rats 1941' medal 'Presented by
Lord Haw   Haw'. An unofficial
medal made by the soldiers. Lord
Haw   Haw broadcast German
propaganda directed at unsettling
the troops defending Tobruk.
John Murray collection.

Mersa Matruh in the Western Desert, Egypt around 1943. AWM MECII77.

Chapter 10

Chapter 10

Our time was finally approaching. Our advance party was being selected and I have no doubt there were many bets laid and much speculation among the junior staff as to who would be given the difficult and dangerous task. Blue Allan, my Brigade Major, was the logical selection, but I confess he was such a good companion I could not face Tobruk without him, despite his inroads into my cigarettes and my liquor (when there was any). So Ian, the Assistant Brigade Major, was chosen and I was woken from my slumber to see him before he went. He looked like nothing on earth. If he had three uniforms he had them all on and, hung round him like a Christmas tree, were binoculars, cameras, water bottles (actually containing water). He looked huge, and as I rolled back onto my humble stretcher, I thought to myself, 'I hope he hasn't far to walk.'

So went our advance party, but we were not destined to catch up with them for many weeks, and meanwhile we had nothing to do but wait. Days later, Blue and I were sitting on a rocky escarpment looking out over the Blue Mediterranean and back to the deserted beach, thinking what a lonely spot it was. Blue fumbled in his scanty clothes and, knowing the signs, I took from my pocket the last of the Mohicans and solemnly broke it in half. How precious was that smoke and, under the influence of his share of it, Blue began to talk about being with a nice girl on some other beach than that one. There was a faraway look in his eyes, which I knew must be somehow quenched, so I said rather crushingly, 'It's not much of a beach, and there's no girl, anyway.' Blue was not deceived — he, of all men, knew my human frailty, but he did not have to speak his thoughts; we understood one another.

Now, at last, our turn actually came. Joyfully we handed over to a British brigade and, in the dead of night, went down to the docks — if you could call what the bombers had left docks. We were ahead of time in our anxiety not to miss the ship. Our men sat on the wharf and, strolling round among them, I heard many comments, mostly about mail, beer, a civilised camp, lettuce and tomatoes and 'won't they be glad to see us'. The night rolled on and still the ship did not come. The men made bets about it, the odds shortening as morning came, and still the ship did not come. Blue and I played double patience and fortified ourselves with Iti cognac contrived from some hidden source of supply; but the ship never came. She had been sunk by the Stukas and we went back to the desert again — this time with nowhere to go. We had handed over, so now we were guests of our relief. How kind they were. A meal appeared from nowhere and, despite their own worries which had been ours for months, their chief concern seemed to be, 'How can we help these fellows?'

We slept till noon, then I rose and girded my loins, saying to Blue, 'Something must be done about this.' So we went to HQ and saw General Scobie, the new General Officer Commanding. 'Murray,' he said, 'I'm awfully sorry for what's happened, but do what you like; live anywhere you choose, and we will do anything we can to help.' My readers may remember General Scobie who had to deal with the recent difficulties in Greece. He said something more then: 'The moon is riding high now. There will be no more ships in for two weeks.' It was the best part of three.

Besides Blue, I still had with me my faithful Hughie and Jack Woolhouse, and elements of the divisional and brigade staffs brought my private party up to about thirty in all. Our first need was a place to live and, in our innocence, we thought we had found it in a couple of deserted Iti huts. The floors were slightly covered with dust, not more than a quarter of an inch deep, the Wilton carpets were conspicuous in their absence, but we had a water frontage some hundred yards away. So comfortable did these quarters seem that we could not understand why they were not already occupied. We were soon to find out. They had been occupied — by a Polish RAP — but the occupants had been shelled out and I found them in one of my wanderings, less comfortable but a good deal safer, in one of the disused Iti gun pits nearby.

So we lived for three weeks in the strangest HQ I have ever occupied — nothing to do, no responsibilities, a prey to anxieties about which we could do nothing at all. Our rocky cranny by the sea was not easy to find, except by one landmark, 'the steps that lead to nowhere'. Once they had led to the portico of a house, but this had been blown to the four winds, leaving the three steps forlornly behind. One day, as I sat solemnly on these steps, I thought of the house that no longer existed and of our own world behind that had been blown away, and our world ahead fraught with doubt and uncertainty. Summoning what courage I had left, I realised that the others must be considered, that something must be found to occupy their minds.

Never, I think, had a progressive bridge tournament been played in such strange circumstances. The cook and I finished up as partners in the final rubber; he wasn't much of a cook either, though a really good soldier of the line, and we lost. His bridge was of that poker variety, but unfortunately our opponents were not intimidated and they called our bluff with dire results for us. We still owe them some Iti, Egyptian, Palestinian or other currency but, having no money anyway, we just left them with their complaints. The cards had become more and more blanketed as night followed night until, in desperation, one opponent, Bert Locke, suggested a dose of Johnson's baby powder. It smelt so fresh, and I heard one of the party who had sprinkled himself and his opposite number freely in the process remark, 'You will have to marry me now!'

The hunt for food was always on, fresh meat seeming but a dream from which I was rudely awakened one day driving along with Hughie to goodness knows where (no doubt to some place where we had no right to be, anyway). The sight that woke me was a couple of gazelles standing pop-eyed or, more correctly, pop-eared, gazing at us from not more than 150 yards away. Not daring to alight, I whispered to Hughie, 'Get your rifle, crawl around the back of the car, and we're right for a week.' But the gazelles were perfectly safe — Hughie had forgotten his rifle. 'Do you mean to tell me,' I asked, my mouth still watering, 'that we are roaming around this place totally unarmed?' Shamefacedly he answered, 'I'm afraid that's the truth of it. I never did like firearms, anyway.'

But this could not go on forever. The moon went down and the ferry began to come again so, without the need for turnstiles or payment of fares, we were to go aboard as guests of our King for a free ride out. This time we really did get aboard, all except my 2/13th Battalion, left behind to catch the next boat (apologies to the Navy — ship) and it was with something of a heavy heart that I thought of them. They were not intended to be used, but things got a little tough after we left, and the 2/13th Battalion was thrown in to capture El Duda. That is history: the charge in the night with bayonets at high port, only lowered when a few feet from the enemy. El Duda fell: who could stop them?

Aboard my ferry I sought out a quiet place and, as we stole out of Tobruk, I felt the need to be alone. I cannot easily describe the thoughts that passed through my mind; looking back into the night, the distant gun flashes made me think first, 'I could help if I was there.' Then I thought of the friends I had left behind forever, their bones to bleach in lonely desert graves. And so, with the steel deck of the destroyer beneath my feet, I looked back over the expanse of the desert that had been our home for so long. I did not think then, but do now, that it stands as a monument to British courage and endurance — one nation against the world, fighting the cause of common justice. And may I be forgiven, as I hope to be, I had those same thoughts at the end of the First World War, thoughts of that free peace which is the right of every man. A hand touched me softly on the elbow: 'Don't you think, Sir, you had better have a bit of sleep?' My ever-faithful Blue, with the uncanny intuition which comes only from intimate association in danger, had rightly guessed my thoughts. I went obediently to bunk, and so, goodbye Tobruk.

When day dawned, we looked forward to our arrival in Alexandria as though it were a bright, new world. The night had been uneventful; the men drowsed or slept, propped up against any stanchion or fitting that would support their bodies and their dreams. Nor was our arrival eventful, except for we who took part. There was no great crowd to meet us, as we had no celebrities on board. I had arrayed myself in the only cloth uniform I possessed and thought to impress General Morshead and his staff, whom I noticed standing on the wharf, and, indeed, the General's welcome was most cordial. Placing both hands on my shoulders, he said, 'You look great, John. Turn right round and let us have a good look at you.' What an embarrassment! My uniform, of which I was so proud, had let me down; so thin had the nether portions become that they literally fell to pieces — a most uncomfortable exposure, though I doubt if anyone minded much.

Having little or no duty to perform in connection with the disembarkation, we went at once to the local club to satisfy the first of our urgent needs with a long, cold beer. I was invited to sit beside the only, and very attractive, nurse present and, although she saw nothing strange in this, I certainly did. I firmly declined. Only the first of my needs had yet been satisfied — I still had not had a bath for about three weeks and, although my best friends would not tell me, I knew. However, continual boiling soon rectified this, but in other ways the desert had left its mark — I was some three stone (19 kilograms) lighter than when we first ventured forth and the clothing that I eventually retrieved from the kit store felt huge.

Alexandria and Cairo did not take up much of our time. Very soon we were off to Palestine. There I learnt that Lieutenant Colonel Burrows of the 2/13th Battalion, which stayed behind in Tobruk, had received a severe wound in the head and been evacuated to a Scottish hospital. On being assured that he would recover, I sent him the cordial message, 'It's a good thing they hit you in the head, otherwise you might have been hurt.'

Our advance party had done its job well and the camp that we were ushered into was complete with all mod cons. On arrival I was given leave, told to go wherever I liked and stay wherever I liked, and my thirst for new places took me to Syria, where the campaign against the Vichy French had already been fought and finished. Damascus and the street called Straight were made to disgorge their treasures, which lie at this moment under window seats and in chests and cupboards in my home — a perfect litter of the wealth of the East. If we ever have to move ...!

We drove over the Lebanons, that high mountain range which rivals Switzerland in its winter sports attraction, put up at the Cedars Hotel, the Mecca for all people in that part of the world seeking distraction, and for months every year totally cut off from the rest of the world by deep snow. Just imagine real snow after the hard, brown, sun-scorched breast of the desert! Amid snowdrifts on top of the highest hill, Blue and I got out of the car and solemnly pelted each other with snowballs in the approved Christmas card style. But this was only a gesture; the cold was too much for our thin blood and we were glad to drop down the mountainside again into Beirut.

I would like to tell here of our abasements, the alcoholic haze we drifted through, the £150 we lost at the races — Syrian pounds, thank goodness (they were only worth two and ten pence of our money). I was actually quite thrilled to see my bill at our excellent Australian club there — fourteen pounds! Syria will not easily forget us, but with a jerk back to reality, we had to return to our job. I confess to being a little the worse for wear on rejoining my brigade, but we had had a wonderful time. Not so the Desert Rats — theirs was still to come.

On my first night home, I was hauled out to a valedictory dinner given by the 2/17th Battalion and, of course, I did the wrong thing again. Noticing a dinner gong cunningly contrived out of an Iti shell case, I remarked that it was pretty good, and was immediately brought to order by Major Johnny Balfe. 'You're not supposed to notice that, Sir,' he said, 'we are going to present it to you later.' A couple of rounds of drinks quickly disposed of any intention I might have had of making a night of it so, making a quick decision, I retired to give the kapok a real thump. But the party went on.

Many hours later, Ian, nobly assisted by two stalwarts of the battalion, bent his weary way home, but not without incident. With arms linked, they staggered through the night, but a sudden storm had turned all the ditches, for which Palestine is famous, into whirling torrents of dark brown water, and one of these suddenly confronted them. However, nothing could stop these three; grasping one another firmly, they chanted, 'One for all and all for one — jump!' right into the middle of the chocolate-brown water. Next morning, with much heaving and pulling, their respective batmen relieved them of their mud-soaked clothing. Our little debauch was over.

Tobruk town seen from the harbour beach. April 1941. AWM OO75IO.

The effect of a thousand pound bomb on a small ship lying in Tobruk Harbour. May 1941. AWM OO7579.

Troops in the desert advance with fixed bayonets.
Tobruk, June 1941. AWM O07972.

The destruction caused by air
raids on the town of Tobruk.
August 1941. AWM 020272.

Major General L. J. Morshead with the new commander of the fortress, Major General R. Mack Scobie, shortly before the Australians moved out. Tobruk, October 1941. AWM 021079.

Major General J. J. Murray with the Governor General, The Duke of Gloucester, after receiving the DSO for his service in Tobruk. Sydney, 16 April 1946. Murray family collection.

Major General JJ Murray on leave in Palestine, 1941, at the ruins
of the Roman city of Jaresh, Trans-Jordan. Author's photograph.

Drawing of Brigadier J. J. Murray's Headquarters at Kilo 89 by G. Maclean.
Now in the Australian War Memorial. December 1940. John Murray collection.

Chapter 11

Chapter 11

Japan had declared war and I was selected, with a number of other senior officers, to return home and assist in our defence. Brigadiers Savige, Close and I were to take the flying boat from Lake Tiberias on Christmas Eve and fly direct (it turned out to be anything but direct) to Australia. My brigade requested that they put on a special parade on the day of my departure, but the rain came down in almost a solid mass, so the parade was off. The last sight I had of the men with whom I had shared so much, and for whom I had so deep an affection, was of them lining the road as I drove off to begin the long journey back. I distinctly heard one of them remark, no doubt with thoughts of family, wife or sweetheart, 'Lucky bastard!'

Ian, Blue, and my batman, Woolhouse, drove with me to see me off. We all felt a bit miserable at the parting and I avoided their eyes as I stepped aboard the small craft that was to ferry me out to the flying boat. Woolhouse said, 'I'd like to make one last request, Sir.' He asked me for the loan for the duration of the war of the old, battle-scarred binoculars that had been his constant companion in the desert. I gave them to him without time limit and hope that he still has them.

We were off. It was cold up top and we tried to keep ourselves warm with the blankets so thoughtfully provided by the flying boat company but, even so, my feet felt as though they were not part of me at all. We were soon to get warm, however; the Middle East was fast being left behind. Right across the centre of India we went from Karachi to Calcutta, then to Rangoon, which had been bombed by the Japanese some days before sending much of the populace to seek refuge in the hills. Here we received the bad news that we could go no further, as Japs were reported to have landed in Sumatra and so were across our route home. There was nothing we could do about it, despite the fact of our having an Air Vice Marshal with us and on his way to take charge of air activities in Singapore, so we were three days in Rangoon before being permitted to get on the move again. They were days not without interest, however. The hotel where we put up was entirely without staff except for one woman — Burmese, I think — though you can never be sure in Burma. It's like the song 'The Road to Mandalay' — white and black have been mating there for years. There was one café still operating, the Silver Grill, and the four of us went there for the strangest New Year's Eve party I have ever attended. The dancers were black, white, and brindle: European women in conventional evening gowns who would have attracted attention anywhere, and seductive half-castes in the kind of dresses one associates with the East. After a couple of drinks, the same thought occurred to all of us simultaneously: to hell with our predicament, let's join the dancers. Partners were not hard to come by and, for the time, we forgot how uncertain were the days immediately ahead.

Next day Stan Savige and I decided would be washing day, and any housewife would have derived much amusement from our preparations. Such things as Blue, Lux, Borax (I've only recently discovered that this list is used in washing) were conspicuously absent; plain soap and water were good enough for us, though the final effect was rather grim. With equally grim determination, we faced the ironing; when either of us had any success at all with any particular garment, he rushed into the other's room and proudly displayed it, while the other guiltily covered up the worst of his ruins. At the end of it Stan surveyed the results of our efforts and moodily remarked, 'We'll just spread the handkerchiefs out on the window sills. They'll dry and iron themselves that way.'

On one of these days we were invited to lunch by General Hutton, then British Commander in Burma. Everyone was very nice to us, but their concern over the weakness of the forces available for the defence of Burma was most evident. The Governor, Dorman Long, whom we visited that evening, was equally concerned. It was quite apparent that, in the face of any determined attack, they would have no chance. And so it proved although, fortunately for us, the proof did not come until after we had left. Apparently the report of the Japs in Sumatra was premature and we were allowed to proceed. We passed over Sumatra and Java and eventually reached Singapore, to be met by several of our officers who formed part of the garrison there. It is strange now, to recall how normal things seemed then, so short a time before Singapore's fall. We had an excellent lunch at the airport, said goodbye to our very good friend and travelling companion, Air Vice Marshal Maltby, and set off again with the flying boat, now filled to capacity with women and children, who were being sent out of the danger zone, some of them to Australia. For the most part they took it very philosophically, despite having left husbands, houses, furniture, and nearly all they possessed, behind them.

At one of our ports of call on the way home, a woman touched me on the elbow and asked, 'Are you married?' She was crying. 'Oh yes,' I replied, 'very much so. Can I help?' 'I'm in great trouble,' she said, 'I have this baby,' (indicating a little two-year-old girl, whom she held by the hand) 'and I'm having another.' This was, rather unnecessarily, to excite my sympathy; I never knew I looked as hard as that. Anyway, it turned out that she had left a small bag containing her letters of credit — in fact, everything she possessed in the world — in one of the cars that had brought us to the hotel for lunch. By phone and car, and thanks to the driver's honesty, the bag was recovered. It became an everyday occurrence for the three of us to be nursing babies on our knees, hushing them to sleep, or, if old enough, telling them stories. We were out of practice at this sort of thing, but their plight deserved our best efforts.

And so we arrived at Darwin, our first Australian port of call. Friends of ours, officers on duty, met us there, but our first greeting was from a number of newspaper reporters, asking us in turn, 'How are you, General?' I said to one, 'What's this "General" business?' 'Don't you know you've all been promoted?' he answered, knowing perfectly well we did not. We turned and, solemnly shaking hands, congratulated one another on this unexpected news.

Next day we flew to Townsville on the east coast. I confess I was anxious to get on to my own home town, Sydney, which we did the following day. I had sent a wire home from Darwin giving the time of my arrival and I could picture my family and friends there to meet me, but it didn't turn out that way. I beat the wire home by two and a half days, to be met by a staff officer from the barracks and some newspaper men only. I immediately excused myself and phoned home, remembering the number without having to consult the book. A strange voice answered and, on my inquiring for Mrs Murray, I was informed, rather coldly I thought, that she was in town shopping. The voice went on to ask, 'Who's speaking?' I thought to myself,

'This will impress her,' and announced, 'General Murray speaking!' Generals were nothing in the life of this, our new maid, so I gave it up and told her very frigidly to ask Mrs Murray if she would be good enough to phone me at my club, receiving an equally frigid, 'Very well,' in reply. I arrived at the club and waited for the call, which came at last. 'Hullo,' I said, and she said, 'Hullo,' and after hulloing each other several times, I said, 'My God, this phone echoes!' Then I heard the words, 'Oh, it is you.' I was home at last.

Major General J.
J. Murray, General
Officer Commanding
Northern Territory
Force, September 1945.
AWM 114871.

Major General J. J. Murray with house staff, Northern
Australia. Author's photograph.

Major General J. J. Murray with the band of the Headquarters,
Northern Territory Force. Author's photograph.

Major General J. J. Murray with the Governor General of Australia,
Lord Gowrie, who made a four week tour of inspection of allied defences
in northern Australia and PNG in 1943. Author's photograph.

Major General J. J. Murray and General Sir Thomas Blamey on visit to
Merauke Airfield in Dutch New Guinea. Author's photograph

Temporary Major General J. J. Murray commanding the Newcastle Covering
Force with Captain John Kennaway, ADC, and Captain Bayne Geikie, Officer
of the Day, Newcastle Headquarters, 1942. Stephen Murray collection

Major General J. J. Murray
reviewing Papuan Troops.
Author's photograph.

Major General J. J. Murray
escorting Field Marshall
Lord Alanbrooke, Chief of
the Imperial General Staff,
during his visit to Darwin
in November 1945. Author's
photograph.

Major General J. J. Murray reviewing troops in Northern Australia. Author's photograph.

Major General J. J. Murray subscribing to the Fourth Victory Loan in Darwin. Mistral Avenue File.

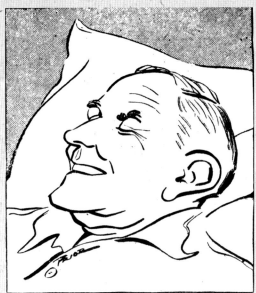

'Soldier': portrait and
sketch by Prior, The
Bulletin, April 1951,
in Concord Hospital.
Amanda Hickey
collection.

John Murray and wife, Madeline, in happier
times, post WW2. Andrew Murray collection.

Epilogue:
A Family Perspective

Andrew Murray

History and character of the memoir

When, as children, we asked our elders what Grandfather had said about the war, the usual reply was 'Uncle Jack (or Dad) didn't talk about the war, unless you mean stories about when he was at the war.'

It is true that Major General John Joseph Murray told his family neither about the horrors of war nor about military strategy and technology. Nor, as he says, did he talk about war in this way when he met with old comrades. Yet he knew a great deal about both these things. He experienced the horrors of trench warfare on the Western Front in the First World War. In the Second World War, his 20th Brigade was in the front line at Tobruk when, and with knowledge gained in the previous war, Allied forces repelled an attack by a Panzer division for the first time.

He did, however, tell stories about himself and his fellow soldiers and about the situations in which they found themselves. He spoke of how they coped and of how they related to one another. The stories of this memoir, be they in the context of Ingleburn, Tobruk or the First World War, are told with the humour and human insight typical of Irish-Australian conversation at the time in which he lived. To the casual reader they might appear just as isolated stories, but put together in this memoir, they deserve more serious consideration.

The memoir begins with a dedication to his wife, Madeline, and with his Daily Prayer. He prayed for 'the gift to understand the men with whom I have to deal, their frailties, their doubts, their fears, that together we might find strength to be true to our ideals.' This is the character of the memoir. His ideals were high, but he constantly strove to understand his men and those he served. He measured their reactions in extreme circumstances and tried to ease the difficulties of daily life in order to ensure the health of a strong fighting unit. Closer scrutiny of the memoir reveals his care in selecting what he will tell and what he will not and whom he will name and whom he will not.

The manuscript containing this memoir was, by the author's own admission, written four years after the epic Easter battle of 13 – 14 April 1941 at Tobruk, when Rommel's first attack was repulsed. By this time, Brigadier Murray had been retired from his command in the Middle East due to his age and sent back to Australia to train new recruits. The entry of Japan into the war, however, saw him eventually promoted major general and appointed General Officer Commanding the Northern Territory Force. It was in this capacity that he wrote the memoir 'sitting in a comfortable chair … with the gentle waves of the Timor Sea lapping against the shore.' Fighting continued in Bougainville, but the threat had receded from northern Australia. Germany would surrender in the next month and Japan would surrender in August.

The family always understood that he intended to publish the memoir but, as my father would say, 'stories about the war were not very popular at the time.' Time was not a gift given to John Murray. He died just six years after the end of the war on 23 September 1951 at the age of 59, after serving as Trade Commissioner first to New Zealand and then to Ceylon.

The manuscript, of which there is only a single copy, was typed in upper case on an Army typewriter and corrected by hand. It sat amongst his papers held by his widow, Madeline, but eventually came into the hands of his eldest son, Peter. Two attempts were made to copy and distribute it at least among family members. In the early 70s, I typed it with three sheets of carbon paper on a manual typewriter with all the mistakes of a beginning typist. It was typed again by a secretary in the early 90s, but the computer file was lost, though printed copies had been made. The original manuscript, however, remained intact, sitting in a file in my father's office.

Alongside the manuscript was a file which we call 'the Mistral Avenue File' because his home address '3 Mistral Avenue' was written on it. It contains his own mementos of the war, including his map of Tobruk; two battle reports; poetry written by his driver, Hughie Paterson, and by others; some of his speeches; significant Orders of the Day; leaflets to do with cricket matches, horse races or concerts; dinner menus with signatures of participants; letters and photographs. The Mistral Avenue File is now in the Australian War Memorial Collection with Accession Numbers PR04685-PR04686 and PUB00880-PUB00895. What they show is that, while he did take pride in heroism and particular military achievements, his major interest was in ensuring that the life of the soldiers was as good as it could be, whatever the conditions. Material from the file has been used to supplement this memoir.

The memoir has finally come to light now for three reasons. First, with the death of my father and, before that, of his eldest sister Mary, it became apparent that, unless papers and photographs were placed in an appropriate archive for safe keeping, they would be dispersed among the next generations (grandchildren and great-grandchildren) and effectively lost to the national record. His medals and papers have already been donated to the Australian War Memorial. Secondly, seventy years after the Siege of Tobruk, Australians are more interested in the history of both the Second World War and the Great War. Thirdly, the good services of the Army History Unit have made it possible to publish the memoir.

Origins

John Joseph Murray was born in Sydney on 26 April 1892, the son of John Murray and Margaret Ferrow. His father, also John, had arrived from Tuam in Galway, Ireland, at the age of twenty-four, aboard the *Lochee* on 24 February 1878. In Sydney he joined his brother, Martin, who had arrived in 1866 aboard the *Africana* at the age of fifteen. It is believed that there were other relatives in Sydney. Margaret Ferrow was born in Kiama, NSW, in 1861, the daughter of Henry Ferrow and Anne Cleary. She and John senior were married on 24 May 1883. John worked as a labourer in Sydney and eventually became publican of the Australian Hotel on Cumberland Street in The Rocks. The family later moved to Manly.

John Joseph was the fourth of seven children who, after the custom of the time, were given names that had cycled through generations of the family but which were often shortened: Patrick Francis (Frank), Margaret Anne

(Madge), Henrietta Agnes (Ettie), John Joseph (Jack), Thomas Frederick (Fred), Henry James (Harry) and Edna. He attended school at Saint Patrick's Marist Brothers School, Church Hill, where he was a keen rugby player. After leaving school in 1910, he took a job as a salesman at Anthony Hordern & Sons. At about the same time, he joined Irish Rifles, a Sydney regiment commanded by Sir Hubert Murray. After three years and at the age of twenty-one, he topped his class at the Officers' Training School at Victoria Barracks and, on 16 February 1913, was commissioned as a second lieutenant in the 33rd Infantry Regiment, Citizen Military Force (CMF).[1]

First World War service

Following the outbreak of the First World War, John enlisted in the Australian Imperial Force (AIF) and was appointed to the 5th Reinforcements of the 1st Battalion on 6 March 1915. He was promoted lieutenant on 1 July 1915 and sailed aboard the *Ceramic* for the Middle East. In February 1916, the 53rd Battalion was formed from Gallipoli veterans of the 1st Battalion and fresh reinforcements. John was promoted captain on 12 March 1916. The battalion became part of the 14th Brigade along with the 54th, 55th and 56th Battalions and proceeded to France in June.

The 53rd Battalion first saw action in the battle of Fromelles, when it lost its Commanding Officer and suffered some 625 casualties, including many officers. John served as a company commander and was awarded the Military Cross for his actions. The recommendation from the field read:

At Petillon on 19th/20th July 1916, Captain Murray led his men in the first two waves of the charge into the German trenches. He showed considerable skill and great energy and gallantry in consolidating the enemy's position when captured, and in directing his own company and other troops which came up to his support. Captain Murray held on to his position, although (owing to the withdrawal of the troops on his flank without warning) he was outflanked and almost

---

1   Here I am reliant on family papers kept by Peter Murray and the recollections of John Michael Murray, Amanda Hickey and others, as well as biographical notes in the Mistral Avenue File. See also A. J. Hill, 'Murray, John Joseph (1892 – 1951)', *Australian Dictionary of Biography*, vol. 15, Melbourne University Press, 2000, p. 453.

surrounded and driven in by the enemy's bombers, when our bombers had run short of bombs. The success of this battalion was largely due to the courage and tenacity of this officer. All the other officers in his company were either killed or wounded.[2]

The battalion rotated in and out of the front lines for the rest the war, much of it in the Somme Valley, and saw action at Bullecourt, Polygon Wood, Anvil Wood, Peronne and St Quentin Canal.

Following temporary commands due to the lack of officers, he was promoted major on 3 June 1917. He was second-in-command of the battalion but, prior to the Battle of Peronne, he took command of a company. In this capacity he was awarded the Distinguished Service Order. The recommendation read:

While leading his Company to the Assembly Positions for the attack on Perrone on 1st September 1918, it was ascertained that the enemy had occupied the trenches in force. This Officer with great skill and initiative led his Company to the attack and cleared the Assembly Position after severe hand to hand fighting thus allowing the remainder of the Battalion to take up its position in time for the attack.

Later while advancing under very severe artillery and machine gun fire, his Company was hung up by two very strong unbroken belts of wire; this gallant Officer, at once placing his men under cover, reconnoitred the wire until he found a gap. He then led his Company through, and continued the advance.

During the later stage of the advance, the Battalion was held up by heavy enfilade fire from Mont St. Quentin and Peronne. This Officer at great personal risk supervised the consolidation of the ground won, and by his energy and cheerfulness, undoubtedly inspired his men to great efforts at a time when the casualties were heaviest.

During the whole of the operation this Officer kept Battalion Headquarters continually informed of the situation.[3]

During this war he was also twice mentioned in dispatches.

---

2   Service Record, John Joseph Murray (NX365).
3   Ibid.

On 5 May 1919, John returned to Australia in command of 1,000 battle-worn troops aboard the *Deranha*. During the voyage he established the principle that the men's time was their own as long as the tasks of the necessary working parties and fatigues were fulfilled. This was no doubt appreciated by the men, but was also something that he was proud of and a mark of his command. His AIF appointment was terminated on 25 August 1919. Apart from two photographs kept by his mother and preserved in his sister's family, the family neither holds nor remembers any memorabilia of his First World War experiences.[4]

Family engaged in the First World War

John was not alone among the family at war. Two brothers, Thomas Frederick (Service Number 2097) and Henry James (Service Number 7767), and a first cousin, Edmund (Edward) Martin (Service Number 1207), also fought. Another cousin, Norbert Anthony, the brother of Edmund, was a marine engineer in the Merchant Navy working for the Adelaide Steamship Company.

Edmund was the first to go to war. Born on 8 November 1893, he enlisted on 28 October 1914 and joined the 13th Battalion. Initially, he was in D Company, but he was moved to C Company and, apart from temporary transfers, remained with the company for the remainder of the war. The 13th Battalion had been formed shortly after the beginning of the war and became part of the 4th Brigade under Colonel (later General) John Monash. After six weeks' training, the company boarded the *Ulysses* for the Middle East and arrived in camp in Egypt for further training in early February 1915. On 13 April, the battalion boarded the *Ascot* in Alexandria and spent twelve days travelling to Gallipoli. At 9.30 p.m. on the night of 25 April, B and C Companies boarded a destroyer to be taken to shore. C Company went on to hold a position known as Quinn's Post. Edmund was wounded in

---

4   An authoritative summary of John Joseph Murray's military career appears on the Australian War Memorial website (www.awm.gov.au). Search the collection with the reference GR19135. He also receives mentions in Charles Bean, *Official History of Australia in the War of 1914 – 1918*, vol. III, pp. 388 – 435 and vol. VI, pp. 836 – 837; and 853 – 854.

the foot on 1 May and was transferred to hospital in Alexandria. He returned to Gallipoli on 12 June. He was to have two more stints in hospital, the first for jaundice and the second for dysentery.

After the withdrawal from Gallipoli, the 13th Battalion retrained in Egypt and then sailed to France to take up positions on the Western Front. Edmund rejoined the Battalion on 4 October 1916 on the Voormezeele Line in Flanders near Ypres. The Battalion was to spend the next two years until the end of war on 18 November 1918 engaging in trench warfare along the front and in battles such as Pozières and Bullecourt and in action along the Somme Valley. Edmund's service record indicates that he was hospitalised several times during these two years. On 3 October 1918, Edmund was granted Anzac Leave, special leave for original Gallipoli troops to return to Australia. He claimed that, at the time, he was one of only seven men remaining on active duty of the 959 men of the battalion who had landed at Gallipoli on 25 April 1914. On 29 April 1919, he was discharged from the army as medically unfit.[5]

Thomas Frederick, always known and now remembered as Fred, enlisted on 15 June 1915 and gave his age as twenty-one years and nine months and his occupation as shop assistant. He had spent six months in the Senior Cadets and three years with the Garrison Artillery in the Militia. By 26 June, he was aboard Troopship A40, *Ceramic*, on the way to Egypt for training. His extant letters show a young man full of the excitement of travel and of experiencing new places.[6] After seeing the bright lights of Cairo, he embarked for Gallipoli and joined his Battalion there on 7 August 1915. He was killed in action on 10 or 11 August 1915 at Lone Pine. The story did not, however, end there.

Fred's mother, Margaret, received a telegram from the Department of Defence dated 5 September 1915 stating, 'Regret son Private T. F. Murray wounded between 6th and 9th August. Not reported seriously. No other

5   I am indebted to notes prepared by Paul Murray (Father Campion OFM), Moya Rubenach and Dolores Davis.
6   The letters are reproduced by Nan Bosler in ANZAC: Something to be Proud of , Narrabeen Community Learning Centre, Local History Resource Unit, 1986, pp. 20 – 23.

particulars available. Will immediately advise anything further received.' On 20 September, Margaret wrote to the Attorney-General, The Honourable W. M. Hughes M. P., reminding him that she had worked on his election committee and asking him to find out what had happened to Fred, since she had heard nothing beyond his being wounded. Hughes referred the question to the Minister for Defence. A Court of Enquiry at Tel-el-Kebir on 20 January 1916 concluded that men missing at Lone Pine were unlikely to be alive but that it was too soon for a definite opinion to be recorded. A further Court of Enquiry held in the field in France on 5 June 1916 concluded that he had been killed. Among the evidence is a statement made in Cairo on 23 March 1916 by Lieutenant John Joseph Murray which read:

> I received a letter from England to the effect that No 2097 Pte T. F. Murray (who is my brother) was killed at Lone Pine between the 10th and 11th of August 1915. This letter was written by a soldier in the same unit who saw him killed. It happened immediately. His comrade reports having seen his body after the occurrence. I have sent the letter to his mother.[7]

The youngest brother, Henry, but always called Harry, was, like Fred, a Militia Gunner at the Garrison Artillery at North Head, close to where they lived at Manly. He, too, wanted to enlist in the AIF, but his parents refused consent. Once he turned twenty-one, however, he decided to join and did so on 17 September 1917 at age twenty-one years and four months. There was consternation in the family, and his mother asked John to look after him. Somehow this was managed, and Harry, who was first enlisted as a reinforcement for the 35th Battalion and travelled to Europe via the Panama Canal on the *Nestor*, was transferred to the 53rd Battalion. He joined the 53rd on 27 July 1918 after a trek across France in which he travelled with one unit after another as he moved towards his destination.

Harry's war service was short-lived as he was shot in the shoulder on 1 September 1918. His shoulder was badly damaged, and his family recalls that he was taken to theatre in the field hospital on three consecutive days before the surgeon was sufficiently confident to reconstruct his shoulder

---

7   Service Records, Thomas Frederick Murray (2097).

rather than amputate his arm. A week later, he was invalided to hospital in the United Kingdom. The surgery had been successful and, after convalescence in England, he returned to Australia on a hospital ship via the Suez Canal. He married Rena McFarlane, his pre-war sweetheart on 19 June 1920.[8]

Between the wars

Civilian life saw John return to work at Anthony Hordern & Sons in Sydney in charge of organising their delivery services. Sensing an opportunity, he formed his own company, Associated Transportation Services Ltd, which coordinated the services of independent truck drivers in the delivery of materials for different businesses around the city. It flourished, and he became President of the Modern Transportation Federation and was appointed Chairman of the Transport Advisory Council by the NSW State Government. He was also a member of the Institute of Transport in London and Sydney. It is not surprising that he listed motoring as one of his hobbies. His other hobby, apart from family life, was military art.

John married (Mary) Madeline Cannon at Saint Mary's Cathedral in Sydney on 4 January 1923. Madeline was the daughter of Peter Andrew Cannon, a grazier at Bulgandramine near Narromine in NSW, and Madeline MacDonald. The family home at 3 Mistral Avenue, Mosman, was a wedding gift from Madeline's father. They had five children, Mary Margaret, Peter John, Helen Elizabeth, Paul Frederick and John Michael, who, being born later, was more a sibling of his nieces and nephews. He is mentioned in the memoir as having been born during the Siege of Tobruk. The family remember John Joseph as a genial man of significant presence and broad social relationships.

Between the wars, John continued his involvement with the CMF in the 53rd Infantry Battalion. Subsequent promotion saw him commanding the 56th Battalion from 1925, the 53rd Battalion from 1930 and then the Australian Army Service Corps, 1st Australian Division, from 1934. In 1938 he was promoted Temporary Brigadier and given command of the 9th Infantry Brigade. With the outbreak of the Second World War in September

---

8   I am indebted to papers held by Barbara Murray and to conversations with her, Jean Murray and Claudia James.

1939, he was appointed Fortress Commander, Sydney, and, early in 1940, he took command of the Eastern Command Recruit Training Depot.

Second World War service

John's service in the first part of the Second World War in Australia and in the Middle East is the topic of this memoir and David Coombes provides the context in his Foreword. John enlisted in the 2nd AIF on 4 April 1940 with Service Number NX365, and was appointed brigadier, with the task of forming the 20th Brigade. The brigade comprised the 2/13th and 2/17th Infantry Battalions, formed in Ingleburn, NSW, and the 2/15th Infantry Battalion, formed in Brisbane and added to the brigade later. The story of John's service in the Second World War falls naturally into three sections.

The decision to march two battalions of the 20th Brigade from Ingleburn to Bathurst was a typical 'bright idea' from a man of John's wit and imagination. A delay in embarkation of troops for the Middle East and Europe meant that the brigade had to move to a new camp at Bathurst where it could train in the conduct of large-scale manoeuvres. Why not march? The exercise, in August 1940, was not hard on the men as the four separate columns covered the 128 miles in stages of nine to seventeen miles per day with a rest day near Katoomba. For the most part, the men slept in billets, but camped two nights on the western side of the Blue Mountains. As attested by newspapers of the day, the march turned into a major publicity event, but its key purposes were to test the Brigade's logistical capability and to prepare the units for wartime movement. Transport units had to move equipment daily, cooks had to have food ready when the men arrived at the various stages, and the new wireless radio trucks received their first test. Medical staff and ambulances had to be on hand as they were needed. Inadequacies showed up, to be fixed by further training, but by and large the march was very successful.[9]

---

9   A full photographic record of the march is held in an album titled 'March: Ingleburn – Bathurst, August 1940' at the Bathurst RSL Sub-branch Museum. It includes newspaper cuttings of the day.

In 1941, during the siege of Tobruk, John was the senior brigadier and commanded the fortress three times during absences of the Commander, Major General Morshead. It is clear that he understood the weight of command, not only as it applied to himself, but also as it applied to others, and so we see references in the memoir to his efforts to listen to and to support Morshead. Militarily, his strategy was marked by constant night patrols which, in the barren desert, kept the enemy forces away from the perimeter. Yet, his real interest seems to have been in the men, for he realised that the Army would function well only if the men themselves were functioning well. Hence, we see his interest in social events such as cricket matches and concerts and the care with which he wrote speeches or orders of the day that were intended to keep men intellectually aware of what they were doing and conscious of being a part of the brigade. For his service in Tobruk, he was awarded a bar to his DSO and was mentioned in dispatches.[10]

The 20th Brigade left Tobruk for a well-earned rest in Palestine on 14 November 1941. General Blamey decided to send John back to Australia to engage in a recruitment drive, and he arrived in Sydney on 15 January 1942. However, Japan had entered the war in December and preparations had to be made for the war in the Pacific and for the defence of Australia. He was promoted Temporary Major General and appointed to command the Newcastle Covering Force, which later became the 10th Division. In August he went to Western Australia to command the 4th Division and his rank became permanent. The 4th Division moved to Queensland and, in 1944, he became General Officer Commanding Rear Echelon, First Army, at Mareeba. From March 1945 until January 1946 he was General Officer Commanding the Northern Territory Force and stationed in Darwin, but with responsibilities in Torres Strait and West Papua. Following his demobilisation on 17 January 1946, Blamey wrote to him:

> You had to carry your share of the heat and burden of the day, particularly in North Africa, and although the luck of the game did not give you an opportunity of a field command in the Southwest Pacific fighting, the duties which fell to your lot were very important.

---

10   See numerous mentions in Barton Maughan, Australia in the War of 1939 – 1945, Series 1, vol. 3, Australian War Memorial, Canberra, 1966.

The training of the units who passed through your hands, when they subsequently took part in action, showed how favourably their training had been carried out.

When you took charge in North Queensland there was an immediate improvement in the discipline of the organisation under your control. You have always developed to an excellent degree the goodwill within your command. This is no mean element in obtaining the highest discipline.[11]

Family engaged in the Second World War

When one looks into the involvement of family members in the Second World War, the numbers bring home how vast this mobilisation was. Five of John's nephews enlisted: Thomas Frederick Murray (NX10533) and Norman Patrick Murray (NX98908), sons of Frank; Thomas Frederick Hellmrich (NX33559), son of Madge; Patrick James Murray (NX102100) and Denis John Murray (164209 — Air Force), sons of Henry. John had some contact with them during the war. Thomas Hellmrich was his staff officer in Northern Australia, a close military relationship which would have seen Thomas assisting John with planning, organisation and communication on a daily basis. Patrick Murray was with the Light Horse on Thursday Island and came under his command. We know that they met. Thomas Murray was with the 2/4th Pioneer Battalion which completed jungle training on the Atherton Tablelands and was, for some time, in Northern Australia.[12]

After the war

Although John had put arrangements in place, five years of war had seen his business taken up by others. He sought public office and was appointed to a three-year term as Trade Commissioner to New Zealand (1946 – 1949), where he worked with the High Commissioner, Sir Roden Cutler VC, with whom he had sailed on the *Queen Mary* to the Middle East in 1941. These

11   Letter, General Sir Thomas Blamey, 24 January 1946, Mistral Avenue File.
12   I am indebted to Barbara Murray, Amanda Hickey and Michael Hickey as well as to the web resources of the Australian War Memorial and the Department of Veteran Affairs.

were good years and the family, apart from Peter and Helen who remained in Sydney, stayed with him. At the conclusion of his term, John was appointed in the same capacity to Ceylon in 1949.

John returned to Sydney before the conclusion of this appointment due to ill health and died on 8 September 1951 in Concord Repatriation Hospital. His funeral with full military honours at Saint Mary's Cathedral was celebrated by Bishop Eris O'Brien and Cardinal Norman Gilroy presided. General Sir Leslie Morshead was one of the pall bearers. He was buried at French's Forest Cemetery.

The cost of service

There were significant family costs to military service. I was with my Grandmother on her fiftieth wedding anniversary and she pointed out to me that she had been a widow for twenty-three years and that her husband had been away at war for five of the years that he was alive. This was tragic, because John Joseph's death deprived her of the company of the man she loved and of the richer life that his generous and gregarious character would have brought her.

All of his children missed him in their growing years and his grandchildren never knew him. His youngest son, John Michael, who was aged ten when his father died, penned this poem some eighteen years later:

My Father,
an enigma, a man unknown to me,
    he died when I was ten.
That night he died, I lay in bed and cried;
I would not be consoled,
    I must express in bitter tears
    my hurt and loss, confusion.
And I have cried again since,
    not so much for him,
    but for what I lost
    not to share my life with him.

And Yet I know him well,
    he is the archetype hero of my dreams,
        the Great Man –
high in achievement, rank and dignity,
respected and loved (and sometimes a little feared)
by his fellow man,
        but along with achievement,
a deep and warm humanity,
an understanding of life
and a sense of humour,
a mischievous twinkle in the eye,
as mother scolds us both for being too long about my bath –
    boys must play,
    father in mid-fifties, son but five,
    bounced up and down in my pyjama pants.
    And how we used to race
    to break the glass surface of the pool
    for our pre-breakfast Colombo swim.

My sister speaks of him with pride and love,
    perhaps too much;
my brother treasures time with him as precious;
    years and a body tattered by wars.
My mother, dipping into wisdom, tells me I am like him –
    I have his faults, I have his strengths.
I wonder at myself, where did I come from?
From him? – How else explain my seeming sanity?
Is he so distant from me?
    Is he within me?
    Am I – in some little way – him again?
        I pray so,
to be an honest, loving, human man like him.

The family bore other costs. The death of Fred at Gallipoli clearly touched the family deeply and two of his nephews born shortly after his death carried his name. Harry was never able to lift his injured arm above shoulder height, although he lived a long life farming as a soldier-settler and father of nine near Griffith. Edmund also lived a long life and raised a family of four, who recall him on occasion yelling out during nightmares, 'They're coming over!' They also recall that he neither talked about the war nor marched on Anzac Day. He had had enough of those memories. After the Second World War, Thomas and Norman Murray returned to find their widowed mother dying of cancer. They stayed with her till she died, but the impact of war and her death had them go their separate ways, unknown to each other for the rest of their lives and, apart from a late brief moment of contact, unknown to the rest of the family.

John carried the weight of war with remarkable stoicism. Although he enjoyed soldiering and spent many years in the CMF, war itself was clearly a necessity that he would rather do without, even if he did not complain. Among his papers, pride of place was given to various Special Orders of the Day recognising the end of a campaign or of war itself in one theatre or another. His real interest was in the men who served under him. In his dealings with them he was intensely aware of their strengths and weaknesses, of what they knew or did not know, of their feelings in situations that might be unfamiliar, confusing and dangerous. His memoir gives testimony to this.

Appendix 1

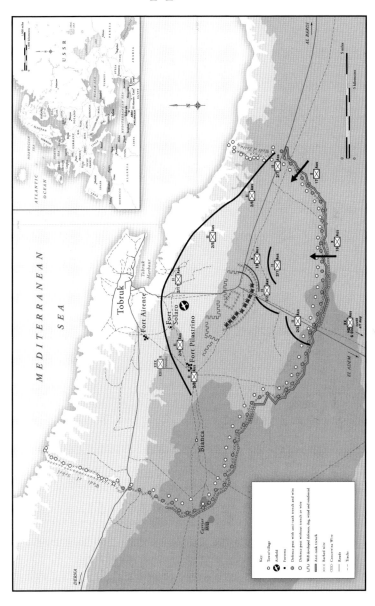

Map 1. Allied assault on Tobruk. Disposition at completion of first day, 21 January 1941.

Appendix 2

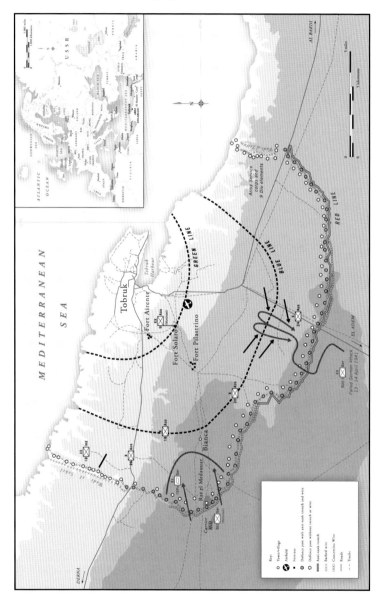

Map 2. Tobruk defences showing German attack, 13-14 April 1941 and main German/Italian attack capturing 'the salient', 30 April-3 May 1941.

Appendix 3

A selection of Major General Murray's Speeches

Address by GOC 4th Australia Division to Officers and NCOs of 13th Australian Infantry Brigade, 8 February 1943

The following is a report of the address by Major General J. J. Murray, DSO, MC, VD, to officers and NCOs of 13 Australian Infantry Brigade Group prior to departure from his command. The address was NOT recorded verbatim.

Opening Remarks

Your brigade is now passing from my command, but I feel I would be doing less than my duty if I did not pass on my experiences so that those in turn may help you in commanding your sections, platoons and companies and so on.

You will remember that, in assuming command as General Officer Commanding the 4th Division, I was particularly insistent that the junior leaders be left with their own men as much as possible. On going round among the units I received many diverse answers on questioning leaders as to whether these were their own men. In many cases it was NOT so and in the early stages there was not sufficient effort to keep sub-units together. Later this was a good deal rectified. It should be clear that if a commander wishes to be successful, he must command his men in all places. You must be with them always, in their work and in their play.

Initiative

Before proceeding to the domestic and man-management side I would like to clarify a few of those things that are so often misunderstood.

Initiative is often taken to mean a reason for disobeying or altering orders, but experience has shown there is plenty of scope for real initiative within the actual orders themselves. It must be borne always in mind that the letter and spirit of orders must not be changed — keep in mind the derivation of the word itself, 'initio' — *I begin* — but begin based on your command orders. As an illustration, if your Brigade Commander orders that the piece of ground for 1,000 yards outside the wire belongs to us and must be denied to the enemy then surely within the scope of that order there is plenty of room for initiative.

And initiative too, means sticking to your job, whatever comes. It doesn't mean that if the going becomes hard that one retires to some more secure place. It means for each of us, I will carry out my commander's orders, carry out his wishes, fight on, do the job I intended to do.

Man-management

For the most part, extremely young soldiers as junior leaders are not experienced in the handling of men. This inexperience is expressed in many ways, often in pride in himself and his rank, forgetting that pride in his unit is the only thing that matters.

Your attitude to your men must always express complete justice. Injustice and favouritism, however small, is very quickly resented. You must remember that as the commander of a sub-unit or unit you are in the position of a high judge to your men.

Show a great understanding of the man himself, of his difficulties, and to do so you must know him. Get to know him quickly. It is your privilege to know and to share his hardships. Put his interests before your own, make them your own.

Training

Just to touch briefly on training, particularly in regard to the care of equipment. In every unit you will meet the fellow who is careless of himself and his equipment; he takes no care of his arms probably because he is inefficient in their use. He doesn't realise what a good friend his weapon can be. He must be taught to like it, to care for it, and to realise that on his care of it may depend his own life, more the safety of his whole section.

Physical Fitness

Physical fitness has always meant a lot, but in this war you just cannot do without it. There are many things which prevent 100% fitness. Among them is the improper use of alcohol. But in this regard do not be intolerant. If you don't drink it may be because you don't like it, or cannot afford it. Remember there are many that both like and can afford it. So, again, be tolerant but see that alcohol is used at the right time and that its use does not affect the fitness of your men.

The misuse of their spare time may impair their fitness. A man cannot be out all night and ride a bike back in the early hours of the morning and do a good day's work. Sometimes to such occurrences it may be best to turn a blind eye. But be careful of him, see that it does not affect his fitness.

Your duty then is to care for your men as much in their leisure hours as in training periods. Have a regard to their spare time, then, not in a 'sticky beakish' way, but tolerantly and wisely.

Care of the Body

You must remember that we all come from different homes with varying standards and types of home training. It is very essential that you instil the necessity for care of the body in every one of your men — it is your duty to do so.

Recently, I asked for a demonstration of the mobile bath unit. I had a platoon strip and go through the bath so that I could judge its efficiency. As often happens, things did not turn out the best. Much improvement could have been effected in the way of forms for sitting while drying feet, foot boards, foot powder etc. Unless properly used and supervised by officers and NCOs, the best results will not be obtained. Officers and NCOs should be present while the men are using such facilities in order to observe any physical defects and report to the RMO. A clean change at least of underclothes should be available after hot showers.

You should have frequent kit inspections and, in having them, know what to look for. See that the men have not got overweight gear. Ensure they have a supply of soap, clean towel, clean under-linen. They should know how to knit and darn, holes in socks just pulled together are no good and give considerable discomfort. Good boots are essential. Make the inspection a real and informative one.

In some places troops are issued with tommy cookers — as in New Guinea. They must be trained in their use. A stub of candle and a box of matches have proved invaluable often. Remember light and heat are life itself to a soldier. Know how to obtain them and teach your troops — you and your men will not suffer nearly the same privations as you would without them.

Generally, when going into action, soldiers dump their kits in a kit store. How many think to warn their men that, after all, everyone will not come out of the battle and not to leave in their kits obscene literature etc., which could give offence to their next of kin or relations. I have seen this occur and real hurt given.

Certainly before kits are returned they are gone through by the man responsible at the kit store, but this official has not the same intimate knowledge of your men as you have. One of your men, for instance, may be engaged to a nice, decent girl and be writing to another. Such letters found in a kit bag would cause real distress. You can prevent it — in fact it is your job to do so.

Always Your Responsibility

On going around and questioning junior leaders, I generally find that when asked for a state they could perhaps produce a scrap of paper saying where their men were, but information was generally lacking as to what they were doing if away from the platoon. Maybe they were away on a digging job, kitchen fatigue etc. Whatever it is, it is your responsibility. See they do their job properly, that the OC party has no trouble with them.

Do your men know how to behave on leave? Instruct them. Ensure that if a man gets into trouble there are always plenty of his mates to get him out of it. I do not mean to thwart authority, but to take him away to some quiet place where he may rest and do no harm, and eventually return him to camp. A very real mateship will begin and grow if the leader understands his men and instructs them to work as a team.

Take time to give your men instructions to dress. See yourself, too, as others see you. I have seen too many NCOs not well turned out. It is not possible to do one thing yourself and insist on the men doing another. After all, 'Example is the best precept'. You have no right to insist on certain instructions being carried out if you are not prepared to abide by them yourself.

Obedience

Obedience is your first duty and that of your men. Not the unshakable kind of obedience when you are present, but the kind that remains true when you and all authority are away.

Sport

In the matter of sport I am very insistent that the men must play in competitive sports. Very often the junior leader does not feel it necessary to be present, but remember that whether your men are at work or play they are always your interest. At least be present at their sport if you do not participate. Men resent it if an officer is not ready to give a word and cheer of encouragement in their sport.

Your Manner

A lot is said and has been written about developing a sense of humour. You will not be much good without it, nor will you get the best results. A spot of humour at the right place and in the right time may direct events the way you want them to go.

Whatever you do, don't resort to bullying. Men do not like condescension; they like to be talked to as man to man, not as inferiors. Don't call a man 'sonny' or 'laddie'. If you can't remember his name, call him 'soldier' — it's what he is or should be and what he is entitled to be called. Always remember that, whatever your rank, there is in the ranks someone who, given the opportunity, could do the job better than you can.

Religion

Have a full respect for the religious beliefs of your men. Each man has a right to his faith and it is your duty to assist and protect him in this right. He should be enabled to attend the services of the religion to which he belongs. And if he has no religious beliefs it is none of your business. Remember tolerance always brings results.

Letters

How many of you have thought to write to the next of kin of your men when they are sick or have met with an accident? It is not difficult. Just say 'Dear Mr or Mrs Blank, so and so is one of my men,' the rest will follow easily. You will find your trouble will be repaid. Not only will the relative reply to you, but will mention your letter when next writing to your man concerned, and a bond will grow between you because he will feel you have his interest at heart.

Soldiers are careless in letter-writing — they forget to write home or put it off, and in putting it off become unhappy in their mind. Their happiness is your concern. Encourage them to write. Make them happy.

It is the duty of an officer to censor a letter for security reasons only. It is not to afford the opportunity to pry into private affairs and indulge in idle chatter. Apart from security, censorship is inviolate and every officer should respect it.

Cooking

Teach your man how to cook. This pays dividends; cooked rations may come up the line on very rare occasions. Teach them section cooking and you will probably find it a difficult thing to get them to go back to company cooking later.

Loyalty

Loyalty is a qualification absolutely necessary in every soldier. I feel I am not wrong in saying that without it you cannot fight.

Some soldiers have loyalty to their particular NCO or officer. It is not enough. They must be loyal to any, to every leader because he is a leader.

Remember though that there is no 'one way traffic' about loyalty. It must be given in the same way as you receive it. It will be found that where loyalty exists there is no trouble in getting the job done.

Reinforcements

The reception of reinforcements is most important. Too often all ranks look down on them and do not put them in the picture. Actually all should assist to do so to their utmost and make them feel as if they belong.

Often after given a chance to prove themselves you will find reinforcements by their actions poking words back down the throats of those who uttered them. After action, too, many of the original unit are casualties. Reinforcements are brought in to build up the unit. They become the unit. Their reception must make them feel part of it.

Closing Remarks

I don't know for sure where you are going and certainly not where you will end up. But somebody has described soldiering as a life of monotonous hardship interspersed with moments of real danger. I am certain the monotonous hardship will come and it is then that real leadership counts. The moments of real danger will also come; again, real leadership will be required. I am certain too that one day you will fight. Prepare for that day and ensure that you can face with confidence what comes and deal with it.

That is all, but I hope that this talk and my experiences which I have passed on will be of some help in your new role. I wish you every success in the future.

Report on talk by
Major General J.J. Murray
GOC 4 AUST DIV

Armistice Day Address

It is a great pleasure to be with you this evening and to share your rejoicing on this Armistice Day, which marks the end of the great European conflict.

Our minds naturally turn to Britain, that tight little island which has suffered so much and whose people are now delivered from the horrors of bombing, anxiety for their homes and children, and not least from the dark curtain of the blackout.

We remember that they have not seen the normal lighting of their streets for years, have never been free from the thought of screeching air raid sirens and falling bombs.

No words could express our admiration and gratitude for their courage and fortitude, for the example set by them and expressed by their great war leader, Winston Churchill, in his clarion call to the Empire to stand fast and save the world.

With somewhat sobering thoughts we remember that we are still at war; while we have every reason to rejoice on this great day, tomorrow must bring with it a determination that we will not relax but indeed intensify our effort against the remaining enemy, until complete peace and freedom are ours.

Thank you.

GOC's Address to Torres Strait Light Infantry Battalion

It is a great honour to have inspected this battalion today. I must compliment you and your officers on the steady discipline that I see on every side. However, it is not of this that I want to speak particularly, but what you have done and the sacrifice of your people in the preservation of this great country of ours. In the grim days when invasion was so near, the Torres Strait Light Infantry Battalion was created of necessity. You stood ready to defend with the enemy practically at our gate. Thanks to victory of our arms not entirely won yet, I may tell you that we are reasonably assured of a return to the days of peace and contentment. As the direct representative of His Majesty the King in this area, I am privileged to thank you on his behalf for your abundant loyalty that has always been given so readily.

When final victory is ours, I would express my personal wish that peace and happiness will attend you always.

Address to 4th Division Banquette and Soak, 16 September 1944

It is a privilege and an honour to be your guest this evening. I have to thank you, too, for the very excellent card of invitation; I intend to send it home to my family, where it will be retained as a reminder of this evening.

I know that it is not the past you want to hear about, but the future, but it is not out of place to recall something of the Formation during our service together.

It is now over two years since I joined you at the first HQ, Moora. You will remember the area we covered from Dandarragon to Geraldton, the visit of His Excellency, Lord Gowrie, and the ceremonial parades held in his honour.

Then our sojourn in the salubrious delights of Guildford. Perhaps some of you will remember better when the train bypassed Melbourne, almost when you were in sight of your homes.

Then Townsville, where we carved a home in the virgin bush for ourselves. You probably remember the leave bus to Townsville, and how fed up some of you were after your first couple of visits, and preferred to hunt in the bush on your day of recreation.

Then the trek up here. This, perhaps, was one of our most interesting experiences. It is not everyone who can say that they have travelled right up the peninsula overland; it was an achievement, carried out without the loss of a single vehicle.

I think you will agree that, while the first few months at Jacky Jacky were grim, without amenities and building yet another home in the bush, things much improved in the latter part of our stay here. Now, perhaps, we have had sufficient of it, and would welcome a change to more civilised parts, where children play and the bustle of ordinary life goes on about.

I do not, for security reasons, make any promise, but you must draw your own conclusions. I do promise this, however, that if you continue to give the same loyalty to the Formation that you have given in the past (while it may not yet be all you desire), it will not put it back any. Speaking of loyalty, I realise that it is not a one-way traffic — it must go down as well as up. To quote Kipling:

'It's not the individual nor the Army as a whole,
But the everlasting teamwork of every bloody soul.'

I interrupt, I know, the festivities of the evening, but this is one of those rare opportunities that I have to speak to you in your own quarters, when formality is for the moment set aside. It is our duty as soldiers that we must, while we serve, each play his part according to his rank or station. This, I know, you will do, and it will be of the greatest assistance to me in achieving what I hope to do for us all.

In conclusion, I have to thank many of you for personal courtesies to myself, which are outside your ordinary duties as soldiers.

Thank you.

Address by Major General J. J. Murray, DSO, MC, VD, GOC Northern Territory Force to Officers of Headquarters NT Force

Gentlemen,

I have something to say to you concerning the duties of staff officers generally. My remarks will not be directed to any individual personally nor to any particular part of the organisation; they will be my views of what a staff officer should be, looking at the matter, as it were, from the other side of the fence.

Use of Notebooks

I have noticed a far too infrequent use of notebooks. Every officer will, at all times, carry one and will be ready with it whenever he comes to me or to any other senior officer to receive instructions. I am perfectly convinced from long experience that, without taking notes, you cannot be efficient.

I suggest also that it is a good practice occasionally to take your notebook to some quiet place and there take stock of all the things which still have to be done, the things which still must be kept before you for consideration and the contacts you should make, eliminating all those which no longer apply, so that your notes are thus continually revised.

Staff Conferences

In the ordinary course of your duty you will attend many conferences where plans are discussed so that the fullest consideration may be given to them. At these conferences it will be my duty to make decisions, yours afterwards to implement them.

It is vitally important that rumours will not spring from these conferences, for rumours are disturbing to everyone and have a grave effect on efficiency. Accordingly, no officer who attends such a conference will divulge anything that takes place there until a final decision has been made.

Initiative

I am a firm believer that staff officers must use initiative, but the scope of initiative must be closely defined. The word itself comes from the Latin meaning 'I begin'; it does not mean 'I alter' or 'I set aside' and, least of all, 'I bluff'. There is plenty of opportunity for a staff officer to use initiative within the scope of his orders without altering those orders or setting them aside.

Staff to Keep in the Field

Every moment that can be spared from office duties should be spent in the field. It is my opinion that there is no good staff officer who is not first a good regimental officer, and a formation cannot be controlled by people in an office who do not make contact with the people outside to see how their instructions are being put into effect. You must study physically out on the ground itself the results of the instructions you have issued.

Attitude to Regimental Officers

You must regard yourselves as the servants of the regimental officers, not as their natural superiors, and to serve them well you must have frequent contact. When you plan, you must plan to assist them, not to make your own work easy. Too frequently I have found the reverse to be the case, the staff planning to suit their own convenience, not the convenience of those who must carry out their instructions.

Encourage Visits to HQ

My opinion on this matter may be a little unorthodox, but in my view a HQ is not a hush-hush place but somewhere that officers may come to discuss their troubles personally and obtain the utmost assistance from the staff. Accordingly, visits by outside officers should be encouraged; they will lessen the number of telephone conversations and the amount of letter-writing and in the end more will be achieved.

Do Not Be A Post Office

Delays caused by people not doing the utmost they can about every document that comes into their hands must be checked; never be satisfied with merely passing it on to the next authority. When letters come from higher or lower formations or from civilians on matters which cannot be dealt with at once, the correct procedure is not to put the whole matter aside but to acknowledge the letter, and if the machinery works slowly and a final solution is long in coming, then send out an interim report so that the originator of the letter will know how matters stand.

Selection of HQ Personnel

Very often other ranks, and occasionally officers, will decide that the HQ is a good place to be and will approach an officer of the HQ to that end. Sometimes the officer, flattered by this personal approach, will find them a job on the HQ. This is no way for a HQ to be manned; the personnel should be carefully selected, and in making a selection, the whole field should be surveyed so that only the most suitable are chosen.

Schools of Instruction

The policy with regard to schools is this: where vacancies are allotted to us for NCOs or officers to attend schools, we will take the fullest advantage of them, and nominations will be considered in the light of the future use that can be made of the students. I have seen much abuse of this principle and consider it an offence to those who organise the schools. Many protests will be heard from units that the personnel cannot be spared to attend schools, but only in exceptional circumstances will these be listened to for, in the long run, the unit will benefit.

Picture Shows

I am a little diffident in mentioning this matter as it concerns myself personally, but I consider that when a General Officer attends the army picture show all officers present should stand as the party enters the enclosure, and at the conclusion of the show should wait until the party has left before dispersing. Personally, I should like my attendance to be as inconspicuous as possible, but in the interests of the service this respect should be shown.

Conclusion

The essential quality in a staff officer is loyalty: loyalty to your commander or your superior, not only when you agree, but when you disagree with him. This loyalty is not a one-way traffic; you have every right to expect it of me, too, and if an officer is doing his best or is suitable for promotion he has every right to expect my earnest consideration. But this does not mean that I will tolerate inefficiency.

**Major General
Commander NT Force
31 May 45**

Appendix 4

Battle Reports

Report by QX8231 Pte A. J. Potter on Escape from POW Camp Derna

After leaving BARCE, at 2100 hours on Apr. 6, we arrived at a point on the desert road at about 07.00AM. A halt was called to enable the convoy to be completed again, in which time individual fires were made to prepare a cup of tea.

The enemy were first sighted about six miles away on our right flank, as we faced the road on which we had been travelling. Two AFVs were first sighted, followed later by six tanks. Orders were given to prepare for action, which were carried out promptly, our defensive position being the edge of the small rise, about 250 yds to the right of the road. As the transport had been dispersed to the left hand side, our first position was about 300 yds from the neatest MT. Our first indication of hostilities was a ranging shell which landed on the road. The second was shorter and much closer to the MT. My next view of the enemy was an armoured car, with a gun behind, which came at a very fast rate into a fold in the ground about 400 yds to our front. This AFV was then made the target of four heavy Breda Guns manned by AA Crews. They were mounted on Dieselene trucks, and as one truck had broken down, it was being towed by No. 1 Gun.

The enemy brought their gun into action, and after ranging with three shells scored a direct hit to No. 1 Gun with the fourth, and the gun being towed, was hit by the fifth shell. These MT were started on fire by the shells and destroyed. In the meantime, the two other guns were firing, but were unable to get sufficient depression on their guns to hit the enemy. Orders were then given to retire into a fold about 150 yds to our right. While moving back, I could see that the second armoured car had swung round and was almost on our left flank. A number of tanks has formed in line on our front. Six were in line on our right flank, and more vehicles were moving down the road on which the enemy were first sighted. Having moved into the new position, our front was then as facing our original left flank.

Between odd shells which were landing, the C.O. took stock of the situation and explained that although we were hopelessly outnumbered, if the remainder of the convoy should be following, they would hear the action and, possibly, turn about and go the coast road through DERNA. One of the Breda then opened fire on the tanks which went back out of range, and began shelling us. Then some vehicles appeared on the left flank, upon which the other gun opened fire, as well as quite a number of rifles. This produced about forty white flags or cloth of some variety, and at the C.O.'s orders we held our fire, as a man was running up waving something. The C.O. replied with a handkerchief and went out to meet him. Meanwhile quite a number of men were walking towards us with their hands up. We, however, soon realised that they were Englishmen, and were escorted by several of the enemy. They informed us that, hearing the action, they had come to see what was happening, and, as they topped the small rise, they found themselves in front of an armoured car. Then as they were also being fired on by our Breda, had no option but to surrender.

Our enemy while walking down with the prisoners, had fired a white light from a pistol, and all guns ceased fire. Our C.O. was then approached by one of the enemy and asked to surrender, as we were, he informed us, completely surrounded. The C.O. was reluctant to do so, but after asking and being assured of, the care of the wounded etc, ordered us to lay down our arms. The enemy, who we then knew were Germans, fired two white signals from a pistol, and all the tanks went out to the road and continued their journey, leaving the two armoured cars to guard us. I counted eighteen tanks in all as they moved along the road.

Our R.S.M. had been injured by a piece of shrapnel, but after having the wound dressed, was able to walk. One AFV remained behind to bring on the wounded and we were marched about two miles onto a road under escort of the other AFV. The enemy gave us good treatment, supplied us with water, and returned later to see if any wounded had been left behind.

All wounded were moved to hospital as soon as possible and about 1500 hrs we were loaded onto MT and conveyed to a cave in the desert. We were warned by the interpreter about secreting of arms, and also attempting to escape, and then moved into an enclosure which was marked by stones. After being given blankets, cooks were procured from the prisoners and a meal was prepared. We then bedded down for the night and at 10AM had another meal. That morning our captors arrived with the officers' gear in a truck and later in the day they were allowed to select their batman. They were moved by MT at about 1700 hrs to DERNA. At 1900 hrs we got orders to move at once so with what gear we had managed to obtain, started off in a long column. Arrived at DERNA AERODROME about midnight and had our first rest. Fifteen minutes' rest and down the escarpment to the hospital in which grounds we spent the rest of the night. About 0700 hrs on Wednesday 9, we were moved to a group of buildings just on DERNA wall, which had recently been occupied by the RASC and were drafted into various buildings, which were in the charge of the Italians. We were then informed that this was the POW Camp. We were not searched and all we were required to give were our jack knives, and an hour later drew our ration of one tin of Italian bully beef, and one packet of English biscuits. Everything went OK for a few days, the officers being allowed to visit the men for an hour each evening. Church services were held for Easter, and there was always a liberal supply of water, but rations were definitely off. Still as there were quite a number of tins of beef and biscuits etc left by the RASC in various buildings, quite a small store was accumulated by the various parties. M & V which had been blown up and burnt by our engineers was being issued by the Italians at the rate of 1 tin per man per day.

On Sunday 13 Apr I was taken with three other men from HQ Coy to do some cleaning up in DERNA. We returned at 1600 hrs to find that everyone had been taken by MT to BENGHASI. The total numbers, I was told, were 600 Englishmen and 240 Australians, which I knew to be correct, as our names and numbers had been entered in a roll, which had been called several times. The same night the prisoners who had been captured at MECHILI were brought in. They were allowed to sleep the night but next morning had to assemble in a big yard and were searched, quite a lot of personal belongings being taken from them.

Due to the lack of organisation by the Italians, no latrines were dug, and as flies were in millions, and only burnt M & V as ration, dysentery was soon very prevalent. Conditions gradually became worse, and after three prisoners who had been captured in TOBRUK had told me the position of things, I decided to attempt an escape. I had made friends with an Englishman from the Long Range Desert Patrol, and when I suggested an escape, he was very anxious to accompany me. I tried to formulate some plans, and as there were only machine gunners (seven in number) to stop us, decided it worth a go.

Everything planned O.K. and having procured three tins of Italian bully beef and two biscuits, a water bottle each, we laid the zero hour at 2300 hrs on Apr 20. Unfortunately, at sundown, a large German convoy came from BENGHASI and camped right in the area through which we had proposed to go. I could see from our position in the camp an entrance into the foothills, which I assumed was a small wadi. At about 2100 hrs I went outside, and could not see the usual guard with rifle, so decided to go at once. Got our gear and the new course necessitated our walking to 150 yds of the German Camp and then swing left to get behind our Machine Gun guards. This was accomplished without incident and proceeded into the wadi, which turned out to be a quarry. Got about looking for a place to climb out, but it was straight face all the way. After a couple of hours, we managed to reach the top of the quarry, and then had about 1000 ft of escarpment to contend with. At dawn on the 21 we were just on top of the escarpment and overlooking the prison camp, but we found the aerodrome had been extended and we would have quite a long walk to get around it. After walking for some hours we encountered two Arabs but as I had seen Arab spies in the camp, I was very wary. However, they directed us on a road which I knew was in the general direction so, we followed it. Later, the road turned SOUTH, so keeping the aerodrome in sight, and in and out of wadis, we continued.

At sundown that evening, we arrived in sight of the road, and at 2100 hrs, crossed the road about seven kilos from DERNA. We were very tired and disheartened, after having walked so far for so little gain, but pushed on, and about a mile from the road, decided to rest for the night. Sleep was impossible as it was bitterly cold. At daybreak we continued again and after about five hours' walk, arrived at a big wadi (wadi Celigh). Had our first meal after going down to the bottom, and decided to have a couple of hours sleep. Moved on about dawn and having climbed the wadi, walked about two miles, and found an Arab well or tank. We could see the water about 18 ft down, so filling one bottle from the other, we managed to make a rope from a piece of twine, strips from the leg of my trousers, and portion of the tail of Bill's shirt, sufficiently long enough to reach the water. We had quite a good drink, and with water bottles full once again, continued all day without incident, laying a course of South East by the sun so as to eventually come out on the coast. We camped that night in a wadi (Wadi Hamesa) and at daybreak continued, arriving at the coast and mouth of the wadi, at about 0900 hrs. The coast was of high rocky cliffs, so decided to keep on top, as we could see sand dunes in the distance. We got down on the wadi and crossed on a sand bar. There were a few Germans floating in the sea, and also on the shore, due to our Navy no doubt.

We climbed out of the wadi and found good walking after crossing another. At about 1500 hrs we met an Arab who told us there was water and food in the wadi ahead, and pointed in the general direction.

After looking up and down the wadi for about an hour without success, decided to try to find him again, but met an Arab boy who was taking some horses down to water, so we followed him. We found the place to be a sort of oasis, with dates and figs growing, and several wells, which, unfortunately, were very brackish but drinkable. The boy said there were four other soldiers camped in a cave up the wadi. We went up to see who they were and found four Englishman. Two RASC and two signallers attached to the 3rd Hussars. They had been cut off on the top of DERNA PASS and after running their wagon with several others down to the first big wadi, ran them over the side, and walked on. At GAZALA the Germans were ahead of them, and the two RASC coves knowing there was an FSD at BOMBA returned with the idea of getting sufficient food on which to live for some time and see what happened. However, on arriving at BOMBA, all that they found was three tins of oatmeal which had been missed by the Germans. With these tins they had made it back to the wadi, as it was the nearest water. We decided to stay the night with them as there were quite a number of Germans and Italians camped at BOMBA (our first of three bottlenecks on the road). We then learned that an MP Captain and Sergeant and three other men (one of whom had been shot in the wrist and chest) were camped in an old water tank about a mile away. As soon as possible I went to see them and found them trying to obtain an Arab guide to take a note to TOBRUK, and bring back assistance by ship. After some few days everything was arranged, and the Captain and the Sergeant set off with the Arab, who assured them he could get through the enemy lines at BOMBA, and take them on a sandbar, past TIMINI and GAZALA, of which only the Arabs knew. About six days after their departure, the Arab returned with the story that, failing to find the sandbar, they had got past TIMINI and gone inland to GAZALA, but in the night had stumbled on an enemy camp in which were quite a number of dogs.

Just as they were caught, however, an air raid alarm was sounded and in the confusion he escaped and returned, but as to the welfare of his charges he knew nothing. In the meantime, two English RE officers who had escaped from DERNA the night after us had arrived at the tank and were staying there in lieu of the Redcaps. We assumed that there would be a search for the Arab and decided to be very wary for a few days. As nothing in the way of large search parties arrived (small ones being shot by Arabs), I decided to have a go at it myself. The two RE captains then told me of a plan which they had formed. An Arab trader had come through with a flock of sheep and goats, and claiming to have brought them from near TOBRUK via ACROMA, without seeing any Germans at all, as they planned to return by the same route, the two officers dressed as Arabs, would accompany them. They were to take several donkeys, with sufficient food and water for 10 days and upon arrival in TOBRUK would procure a ship and return to make for us a very easy and dramatic rescue. However, as the plan would not be put into action for five or six days and having heard the full report of how many trucks had been dumped over the wadi in which was quite a good quantity of rations, I decided to take a trek back to see what rations were left. Our sole diet of one handful of oatmeal per day was becoming exhausted, and I realised we would have to get rations somewhere, if we were going to see the two captains' plan through. I set out with Bill and one RACS cove to investigate the wadi, but after a day's walk we arrived in the bottom of the wadi only to be informed by an Arab that Germans came down every day and were coming along the wadi now. We climbed that wadi faster than any mountain goat and didn't stop until we were about three miles away. We had to return empty-handed and shorten our already short rations. On 14 May, the two captains started, and we were to give them 10 days if possible, before considering the scheme a failure. We were very restless owing to the fact of short rations, and slight dysentery, and to the fact that each day we waited we were getting weaker all the time. However, as the time was nearly up, and we had made a couple of trips to BOMBA to see how the land lay, we prepared on the night of 24 May to move off. An Arab friend had managed to get a tin of bully beef and an Italian biscuit each from DERNA and with a water bottle each and rations, set off on the morning of 25 May. I had got a rough idea of the nature of the country and the bottlenecks at BOMBA, TIMINI and GAZALA. Bill and myself were to go in the first party, but the two RASC coves wanted to join us, and the other two Tommies were to give us four hours' start, so as we would not be running into each other on the way. We proceeded to BOMBA without event, but as we were about fifty yds from the road to BOMBA head, a truckload of Italians came along. We went to earth as quickly as possible and fortunately were not seen. Just as we were going again another one came back from the main road which was about 200 yds distant. I was half decided to wait for darkness as once we had crossed the road, had an open flat of about 600 yds before any cover was available. But it was essential to get past TIMINI the first night so as to be able to walk to GAZALA the next day. Speed was essential as we knew there were no Arabs from whom we could get assistance, and no water. So we decided to give it a go, and when halfway across the flat, another truck came down the road. Tried hard to get cover behind a camel bush, and thought we had been seen, as the truck had stopped and we could see the Italians were pointing straight at where we lay. The truck then started towards us but after a hundred yards or so turned back onto the road and went to BOMBA head. Needless to say we proceeded with much haste and found a stack of drums that may have been the object at which they were pointing. We carried on and arrived with sight of the first white house at TIMINI half an hour before sundown. I was very glad of a rest as the pace had been fairly brisk, and down on the beach the two Tommies who were to leave after us came along, and I knew then that they had been tailing us all day. As six was too many in one party they promised they would not leave until midnight to give us a chance of getting well ahead. At sundown we started (but as distance is very deceiving in the desert, and night marching damn near impossible), at midnight I could not see any sign of a white house. We kept going, and about 3AM decided to wait for daylight and see the position of things. At dawn I found we were past the first white house, but were within 200 yds of a second around which were camped about 50 German trucks. Some more haste was urgently required, and after going about a mile, discovered two men walking towards us from the right. Thinking they were enemies, we had to get into a swamp and keep going. After an hour's wading arrived at the end and found the two Tommies sitting down and watching us. After very mildly asking why we waded through the swamp, my flow of obscene language was sufficient to change their ideas about tailing us any further. I think they later walked to the road and gave themselves up as their water was just about finished then. Carried on all day and just before sundown came around a bend on the beach, and about 50 yds ahead a party of Italians were cleaning out a well. I had a good look at GAZAIA which was about six miles distant, and tried to form a plan for getting past the white houses. There were quite a few small camps on the flat and I was dubious as to whether I could find a way through them. As darkness came we could see the Italians going into a camp about 50 yds away. Bill went over to an old tractor to see if there was any water in the radiator, but as it had been there for quite a long time, was very oily and rusty. I had a drink but was sick as soon as I had done so. We then decided to try the well, and moving quietly managed to get down O.K. The water was stinking but cool, and not bad to drink. Having finished the remainder of our good water, filled up the bottles and climbed out. However this water again made us sick, so we could only use it to wash out the mouth. As it was now getting late, and not being too sure of my bearings, decided to get on the main road. This we managed without incident, except for the barking of several dogs which caused us to go very carefully.

After walking on the road for an hour or more, I heard a noise behind, thinking it to be a truck in the distance, but found it to be a German on a push bike with the mudguards rattling. We just walked to the side of the road and sat down. He came along, stopped, had a look at us, and after walking about fifty yards, got on the bike again and rode away. We got on the road again and after a few hours with no white house in sight, decided to camp the night, as we were all feeling pretty seedy from the water.

We swung left off the road looking for cover and about 50 yds walk brought us to a German truck. Dodged it and ran into another. After dodging quite a number, we eventually came to a big thorn bush and we scrambled into it. At dawn I had a look around and I nearly had heart failure when I could see the number of trucks we had walked through. Looking left I found another convoy almost as big, within 50 yds of the bush. We got back into the bush and discovered that a road ran just in front of it. This led down to the coast, and about 8AM the first truckload of Italians came along. Several trucks went up and down, also several walking parties, but we remained undiscovered. Shortly after noon everything seemed quiet, so we got out and moved over to a small wadi which led up the side of a rise. On reaching the top discovered quite a few camps and coves walking around, so moved back halfway and waited for darkness. Our first day without water in the hot sun was not pleasant, so we were very anxious to get started. Took a bearing by a star and moved off, and arrived at a road which the RASC coves told me led to a water point. I was tempted to try for some water but hearing dogs barking, decided it was not worth the risk. After walking on for a while, waited for dawn and moved again. As we came over a rise, I could see the coast once again and carried on in that direction, but on the inner edge of some sand dunes, I could see three tents. As it was very early, nobody seemed to be up, so I thought it possible to dodge through the dunes. As we climbed the first one I could see nothing but over the second I nearly walked on top of a camp. It was then that I realised that the whole of the dunes was a large camp, so going as fast as possible, we managed to get clear. On about our second last dune, just as we got to the top, saw two men walking along the bottom going towards the sea.

However, we gave them time to get to the beach then continued. After having so many close calls I was beginning to wonder if our luck could hold as it had done so far. Kept walking, and as my boots were worn out and Bill had none either, the hard going soon started to make our feet sore. About an hour's walk brought us to a German truck parked very close to the shore. We moved up to see if it were possible to get around it. However just as we were going to move to the beach again the truck moved towards us. We hurried into some bushes on top of a dune and the Jerry decided to pull his truck up at the same place. Not daring to move we watched the procedure. He was soon joined by two mates and they decided to have breakfast. The sight of water and coffee made us feel like rushing them. However, after they had had breakfast, a smoke and a yarn, they decided to move on. When the driver got into the truck, I thought he must see us as he looked straight into the bushes, but again Lady Luck favoured us. As soon as possible we moved on again as another truck and car had come down but were behind us, on the opposite side of a few dunes.

On for another couple of miles, when I could see a swimming party and some trucks ahead, it was then nearly noon and getting very hot. We had just passed three mines washed upon the beach, when I could see two men walking along the beach towards us. We moved up the bank and took cover behind a few camel bushes. It was not very long before we found the object of the two strollers was to use the mines as targets for rifles. Fortunately the mines were duds, but we had a few close calls from bullets that were ricocheting, some being much too close for comfort.

As this was our second day in the sun without water, we were hoping the Jerries would get an urgent call somewhere, but they kept coming down by the truckload, so we had no option but to wait for dark. At sundown a few trucks came and parked about two miles away from the beach. Bill decided to try to tap one of their radiators for water, so as soon as it was dark enough, we went up to within 50 yds of the truck selected. Bill went forward, and, as he told me later, he had just started to get things going when a Jerry got out of the truck and saw his foot. He yelled out something, and went for a gun, so Bill up and went for the lick of his life. I lay quiet for a while to see what was going to happen and later moved back to the beach, but couldn't locate Bill. Walked around all night trying to locate him, as I did not think that he had been caught. At daylight, failing to find him, moved on again, and a couple of miles up the beach found an old towel he had had wrapped around his foot, so I knew he was O.K. and had gone on.

Our tongues were swelling fast, and I knew it would be almost impossible to lay up another day in the sun without water. Just as the sun began to rise we walked around another small bay and could see we were right on a large German Signal Camp. I kept going and as it was a shelving beach, some of the tents were so close I could have spat on the men sleeping in them.

A sentry was marching up and down outside a big tent 50 yds away. He stopped and looked at us, and I thought it was certain he would halt us, but he turned and walked along his beat. Looking straight ahead all the while, I kept going and could see him looking at us again. As we had 150 yds or more to cover before we were out of sight, I cannot explain why he did not recognise us. I was dressed in F.S. battle dress and was carrying my hat. The Tommies were in their battle dress, wearing forage caps, and one a driver's cap. Continued on, and came to a blind wadi in which I could see quite a number of Arab tents. I did not want to go in as I thought it too risky as there was a big German camp on top of the wadi. However one of the Tommies could not resist the cool waters of the Mediterranean, and started drinking it. I pulled him out and brought him around, but I knew he was bordering on the stage of madness and water was essential, so into the wadi we went. Met an Arab and being unable to talk, pointed to my tongue. He told me he was a Senussi and I knew he would give us every assistance possible. He hid us in an old tank and later brought some Arab bread, a small dish of olive oil, and a small pot of tea plus water. Having eaten the bread and olive oil, we had a couple of hours of much-needed sleep, and discovered the swelling in the tongue to have almost gone. After sundown the Arab came back again and said that after we had a meal he would show us the way. He led us to some saltbush away from the camp and there produced the meal. What it was made from I don't know, but it was as hot as the flames of hell, and of all things, it was served up in a pot, handle and all. After the meal he gave me a packet of cigarettes and I have never enjoyed a cigarette so much in all my life. Then we proceeded on the last lap of our journey. The Arab told us we had about ten miles to go, and eleven wadis to cross. Once we had crossed eight, he said, that was the end of the Germans' lines, and the eleventh was English. Also, to keep to the coast as the Germans moved back every night. We carried on as quickly as possible, but owing to the fact that one chap had a very bad tendon in his leg, had to break the pace down.

Eventually came to the wadis and his leg became so bad that he had to be given assistance. After climbing wadi after wadi, arrived at a fairly deep and wide one. I had miscounted one and thought it to be the tenth, and as we were crossing the bottom daylight started to break. I was almost on the wire before I saw it, and we had just got around the end and were going to start climbing a hill of sand when I heard someone call out Halt. I looked up and could see a man with the sights of a machine gun right on me. I sang out that I was an Australian and unarmed. He started to jabber something and not wishing to be shot I yelled again good and loud. I could see a man running along the top of the wadi some distance away and also heard him sing out. At last a voice from the top said 'You are Australian.' I said 'Yes.' He said, 'We are Indians' and came down to assist up to the top. At last we knew we were once again in friendly hands after being 41 days in the desert.

Signed: Pte. A.J. Potter.

Report on Movements and action of Tank Guiding Party, night 9/10 October 41 — Party consisting Capt. McMaster, Lieut. Sabine and Sgt. Polson

When the leading tank reached R.50 at approx 2000 hours, with Lieut Sabine I joined Sgt Polson and walking ahead of the tanks proceeded to guide them through the wire. The tanks were then moving at approx 1½ mph and making considerable noise. When the 5th tank had cleared the wire they stopped and I contacted the Tank Comd who was in the third tank to check up on the bearings that we were taking for PLONK. When the Tank Comd was informed of the amount of noise the tanks were making and the distance at which they could be heard he was most disappointed as he appeared to think he was moving very very quietly.

The Tank Comd then asked whether that, as all chance of surprise now appeared to be gone, it would not be better for them to remain just outside the wire and 'rush out' at anything that appeared rather than move out to PLONK. However, when it was pointed out that he would probably be too far away for effective action if anything was reported in the vicinity of PLONK, he decided to move out there according to the original plan.

The tanks then moved off on a bearing of 222 deg from the gap at R.53 at approx 1mph, with myself and Lieut Sabine in front as guides and Sgt Polson riding on the Comd's tank as a runner for the Tank Comd.

At 2100 hrs, 15 'I' tanks and two light tanks had cleared our wire and were moving in line ahead approx 20 to 30 feet apart in the direction of BIR EL AZAZI (PLONK).

We moved at this dead slow pace for 700 yds when two figures appeared coming towards us. I contacted them and when I first spoke to them could not get any answers to my questions and for a moment thought I had picked up a couple of 'Dagoes'. However, after a little persuasion, one was able to answer and told me that he had just escaped from BONDI and that the xxx!!s had surrounded the place with tanks and infantry. He also stated that he and his mate were from 'A' Coy of 2nd Queens. I stopped the tanks and the Tank Comd interrogated the Tommies (or at least one of them as, throughout the whole of the time they were with us, the second one never spoke).

The Tank Comd then suggested that he go straight for BONDI, but as none of us were in a position to act as guide and the two Tommies appeared to have not the faintest idea of how to get back there, he decided to continue to PLONK, but to do so at full speed. Time was now approx. 2130 hrs.

With Lieut Sabine we mounted the front of the leading tank and headed at full speed for PLONK; when travelling at this speed the tanks were still in line but approx 300 yds apart. It was now extremely difficult to keep on our bearing and we passed by PLONK about 300 yds to the SE. Fortunately Lieut Sabine silhouetted PLONK in the moonlight about 500 yds to our right rear, and we turned and headed for it arriving there at approx 2205 hrs.

On reaching PLONK I contacted the Cpl in charge of the PLONK patrol who informed me that there had been heavy shelling on that area and that his Sgt had had to return to our own lines suffering from shell shock, otherwise there had been nothing seen or heard out there. Capt. Brien was then contacted by phone and asked for information regarding reports of BONDI. After about 5 minutes the Adjt of the 2nd Queens telephoned me to say that the last contact they had had with BONDI was at 2100 hrs and that the place was then surrounded by tanks and some infantry. This news was passed to the Tank Comd who decided to move at once towards BONDI on a bearing of 140 deg. The tanks were then all to the SE of PLONK and from the slightly higher ground we were on, this long line of grey shapes made a magnificent sight in the moonlight and one which none who were fortunate enough to see it will be likely to forget.

After the Tank Comd had left me to return to his tanks we heard sounds of enemy tanks to the SE; this information was at once sent to the Tank Comd whose only reply was 'Good.' Approx 5 minutes later our tanks turned and moved off in a south-easterly direction. They had not been gone more than 3 minutes when Capt Brien phoned that Col. Crawford had information of an enemy minefield 3000 paces on a bearing of 207 deg from PLONK and asked me to pass this on to the tanks. At this moment one 'I' tank was seen returning towards us and when it reached PLONK we were able to pass this news to the Tank Comd by wireless. This tank which returned to PLONK did so because of slight engine trouble and it holed up on the left slope of the centre mound; the comd of this tank took an extremely poor view of being left there by himself.

At this time the sound of our own tanks moving away was very loud but at the same time other sounds were heard on our front. Sgt Polson suggested these sounds were only echo but it was apparent a few minutes later that they were anything but echo and that there were enemy tanks approaching us from our right front. I reported to Capt Brien that a foreign element was being introduced to the proceedings and a few minutes later 3 enemy tanks could be seen approaching from the SSW; a 4th was reported but I could not confirm this. When first sighted these tanks were approx 300 yds away. When they had approached to within about 200 yds I reported to Capt Brien that the position appeared to be getting a bit serious and he ordered us to retire.

The Cpl in charge of the PLONK patrol got his men together and started to move back along the telephone line, waiting about 50 yds in my rear, also Lieut Sabine. At this moment our own tanks which had moved off to the left evidently made contact with the enemy as sounds of heavy fire of MMGs and 2- pounders could be heard and a lot of tracer commenced to fly about. This I reported to my Coy Comd before disconnecting the telephone, and also that if he did not wish a ball by ball description of a tank battle I was off.

Sgt Polson, who was beside me, then pointed out that the enemy tanks to our front had stopped about 200 yds out, having evidently sighted our lonely 'I' tank that was at PLONK. These enemy tanks then started, one going to the right, one remaining where it was and one to the left and were quite plainly going to surround PLONK and the 'I' tank there. At this stage no fire had been opened by either side. Polson and myself then disconnected the phone and moved back with the PLONK patrol. We had gone about 100 yds when fire broke out in our rear, both heavy MG and 2-pounder and it was evident that the enemy tanks were attacking our own.

After retiring about 350 yds, heads were counted and Lieut Sabine reported that we were minus the two Tommies from BONDI who, on reaching PLONK, we had tacked on to the PLONK patrol. It was then remembered that they had been last seen disappearing into a cave when the enemy tanks approached and in the excitement of leaving they had been forgotten.

Col Conway immediately volunteered to return and get them. However, ordering Lieut Sabine to take the telephone and report our movements through to Coy, with Sgt Polson and Cpl Conway I returned in the direction of PLONK. When about halfway back I found we had an extra man with us and when I asked him what he was doing he said he had left his b…y haversack there and no other b…d was going to get it. We reached PLONK and Cpl Conway dug the Tommies out of the cave and after putting them on the phone line and telling them to go like hell we, with some difficulty, were able to get them moving. At this time it could be seen that the two enemy tanks which had moved to the flank were firing at the 'I' tank from which their shots could be plainly seen ricocheting and the third tank had approached right up the centre of the sand dunes and was within approx 30 yds of the 'I' tank and firing point blank at it, and about 50 yds from us. We waited and saw the 'I' tank fire back at least once and score a hit on the enemy tank which, however, continued to move towards us.

Things were then pretty thick so we started to withdraw. However, we were evidently sighted by the centre tank and had not gone more than a few yards when we were opened upon by fire from this tank. The moon was then obscured by cloud for a few minutes and we were able to make the most of that and move back in bounds until we contacted Lieut Sabine and the patrol who had also been pinned down by the fire directed at us. We then cut the telephone wire and with the Tommies in the centre moved back to our own lines arriving there without loss.

The sounds of the tank battle to the SOUTH continued until we were within about 300 yds of our own line when tanks could be heard moving in the direction of PLONK and which we took to be our own tanks.

REMARKS

1. Our tanks could be heard moving at a considerable distance and it was noticed by our forward posts that more noise was heard when they were going slowly than when the pace was increased.

2. The Tank Comd appeared to me to make a slight error in judgement in not leaving more tanks at PLONK when he moved SOUTH.

3. The main body of tanks returned to our lines too early as, if they had not, they would have probably got the crippled enemy tank that was laid up for some hours to the EAST of PLONK.

4. I would like to say that the conduct and coolness of Sgt Polson and Cpl Conway on our return to PLONK was outstanding.

5. The main tank battle appeared to take place 1000 to 1500 yds EAST of PLONK.

6. One shot from the 2-pounder of our 'I' tank was seen to ricochet off the enemy tank when the range was only 30 yds.

Ian F. McMaster Capt.
2 i/c A Comp 2/17.

Appendix 5

Original Documents

SECRET

HQ 20 Aust Inf Bde,
In the Field,
29 Jul 41.

<u>TO BE DESTROYED AFTER READING</u>

2/13 Aust Inf Bn
2/15 Aust Inf Bn
2/17 Aust Inf Bn.

<u>ENEMY   MORALE</u>

Information is to the effect that at the moment
the morale of the enemy facing the perimeter is very
low, particularly that of the ITALIANS.

The letter "V" already has a big significance
and for your convenience the attached pamphlets are
issued.

The Bde Comd directs that these will be placed
by the use of clips, string, nails, pins, etc., to
bodies, posts, wire, sand bags, sangars, etc, by your
patrols.

Care will be exercised that the placing of the
pamphlets is not the primary role of the patrol, but
incidental to its usual operations.

The Bde Comd further directs that the pamphlets
are not to be used indiscriminately but placed where
they will have the desired effect.

(H. T. ALLAN) Maj
BM 20 Aust Inf Bde

NX 365,
Brig J. J. Murray,
HQ 20 Aust Inf Bde,
Australian Imperial Force,
ABROAD
14th June 1941.

Mrs. W. Kierath,
Bokhara,
NARROMINE.

Dear Mrs. Kierath,

I write to extend my very deep sympathy in the loss of your son Greg. The fact that he had such a gallant end in the face of the enemy does not compensate for the loss to you and your family in the first place, and to his friends here in the Brigade secondly.

I can say without hesitation that there was no Officer on the staff of whom we were more fond and proud. He was buried with great reverence in the cemetery here and I am having photographs taken which we hope to develope and send to you if and when we are relieved.

I do appreciate your great grief and feel for you deeply.

Kindest regards,

Sympathetically yours,

Brig

Comd 20 Aust Inf Bde

ORDER   OF   THE   DAY

By

Brigadier J. J. MURRAY, D.S.O., M.C., V.D.
Commanding 20 Australian Infantry Brigade, A.I.F.

————————————

Tobruch, 20th October 1941.

    We have the honour to be the last Brigade to leave
Tobruch. It is a tribute to your efficiency. Each of
you has given to the defence of this Fortress the full
extent of your skill, courage and endurance, without
which it would have been impossible to hold it. A
very high standard has been set and we must keep that
standard.

    In the days that lie ahead you may be assured that
every effort will be made to ensure for you a well
earned rest, with the fullest possible amenities. It
is confidently expected that on the journey out to our
destination the Brigade will move with the perfect
discipline that has characterised our previous operations.

    Before coming to Libya we were a Brigade under training,
untried, but we now have a tradition to preserve. Many
of our men have died to make this tradition and they remain
in Tobruch. Remember them, for their honour and your own
is in the keeping of every single soldier of the Brigade.

Brigadier

HQ 4 Aust Div (AIF)

25 Apr 44

ANZAC DAY

ORDER OF THE DAY

by

Major-General J.J. MURRAY, DSO, MC, VD

To-day 29 years ago saw from a soldier's point of view the birth of our Australian nation. In commemorating the day our thoughts must go back to our gallant dead, who died in that day's battle and subsequent actions in that war and the present conflict.

They gave us all that we hold dear. Let each of us resolve that by no word or deed of ours will we tarnish the heritage that has been so proudly passed to us.

Our duty is very clear. Every Australian soldier held prisoner must and will be released. There is to be no rest until our common enemy is utterly and absolutely defeated. When this is accomplished it will be our privilege to make this our own Australia, an even better and happier place for those of our own and future generations whatever their rank or station.

(J.J. Murray)..Maj-Gen
COMD 4 AUST DIV

AUSTRALIAN MILITARY FORCES

ORDER OF THE DAY

BY

GENERAL SIR THOMAS BLAMEY,
COMMANDER-IN-CHIEF

Headquarters,
Australian Military Forces.
9th May, 1945.

END OF THE WAR IN EUROPE

The war in Europe ended this morning.

The people of the Allied Nations lift their voices in gladness and thanksgiving wherever they may be. Our armies have won complete victory over German tyranny.

Our Allied effort will be concentrated now on the last enemy of civilization—the Japanese. He has been defeated time and time again and now our hosts are already assembling to his complete destruction.

I send greetings and congratulations—

First: To all those of the A.I.F. who fought in Europe and the Middle East. They took a full share of the strain in the hardest early days and helped to lay the foundation of victory.

Second: I send greetings and congratulations to all ranks of the Australian Army. Again, they took a full share of the early strain against the Japanese, and again their efforts are bearing them on to final victory.

We tender a tribute of comradeship to those who will never return and we vow ourselves anew in their name to compass the final destruction of civilization's last enemy—the Japanese.

General,
Commander-in-Chief,
AUSTRALIAN MILITARY FORCES.

AUSTRALIAN MILITARY FORCES

ORDER OF THE DAY

by GENERAL SIR THOMAS BLAMEY,
Commander-in-Chief

Advanced LHQ, Borneo,
15th August, 1945.

SURRENDER OF JAPANESE.

The Japanese have surrendered.
Our long and arduous struggle has ended in complete victory.

The climax has come at the time when all six Australian Divisions are fighting strenuously, each on its own area, in the far flung battle lines. No divisions amongst the Allies have contributed more to the downfall of our enemies than ours.

Our general officers and our commanders of all grades, our regimental officers and our warrant and non-commissioned officers have led you unfalteringly to victory. Under their guidance, the troops have been formed into a magnificent army to the pride and glory of Australia.

We have fought through the burning days and freezing nights of the desert. We have fought through the ooze and sweat of tropical jungles. We have defeated the Italians and the Germans and we would soon have destroyed completely the Japanese before us.

We are now to go to our homes, having done our part in ensuring freedom for all peoples. We will not forget this freedom, for which we have fought so long and successfully, and so let us stand together in future years to ensure that it remains the crowning heritage of Australian people. Above all, we give thanks to the Almighty for His greatest and crowning mercy that marks for all people the total downfall of tyranny.

General,
Commander-in-Chief,
AUSTRALIAN MILITARY FORCES.

C.8287/45.

SPECIAL ORDER OF THE DAY

by

MAJOR GENERAL J. J. MURRAY, DSO, MC, VD

Commanding

NORTHERN TERRITORY FORCE

―――――――

By divine providence and the courage of our arms we have overcome that which assailed the peace of the world, and we have now the vast responsibility of creating a new heart superseding passion, selfishness and greed to build a new world where common justice will transcend every emotion.

We should be deeply grateful to those who lie in the waste spaces of the four corners of the earth with their sightless eyes turned to heaven, for their sacrifice is the price of our freedom.

Let no one forget his obligations. Each and every action of ours should be in service and not in gain, for true happiness lies only in service.

J. J. Murray,

Major General,

COMMANDING

NORTHERN TERRITORY FORCE.

. . . .**1945**

AAF A 20E (REV. JUN. '45)

Certificate No 21654

Australian Military Forces

Certificate of Service of an Officer

This is to Certify that

NX365 Colonel (Temporary Major General) John Joseph MURRAY DSO.MC.VD.MID.

Headquarters 4 Aust Division

Served on Continuous Full Time War Service in the

Australian Imperial Force from 4 Apr 1940 to 6 Jan 1942
Citizen Military Forces from 7 Jan 1942 to 28 Dec 1942
Australian Imperial Force from 29 Dec 1942 to 16 Jan 1946

for a Total Effective Period

of Two thousand one hundred and fourteen Days

which included Active Service

In Australia for 1338 days Outside Australia for 481 days
Service in the Ranks (included in above) was
from NIL to NIL
Honours, Decorations and Awards during that Service

BAR TO DISTINGUISHED SERVICE ORDER (London Gazette 8176) 30.12.41
MENTIONED IN DESPATCHES

War Badge R.A.S. No. A.293358

Full Time War Service as an Officer in the

Australian Imperial Force ceased on 16 Jan 1946

Place Sydney O J Fraser Lt for Lt.Col.

Date 16 Jan 46 Officer in Charge N.S.W. Ech. & Rec.

Description of Officer on Completion of Service

Height 5 ft 11½ ins. Eyes Brown Complexion Medium Hair Grey

Marks or Scars NIL

Specimen Signature of Officer

* "EFFECTIVE PERIOD" MEANS THE PERIOD OF SERVICE, LESS ANY CONSECUTIVE 21 DAYS OR MORE FOR WHICH THE OFFICER WAS NOT ENTITLED TO PAY.
† "AUSTRALIA" MEANS THE MAINLAND OF AUSTRALIA AND TASMANIA. ≠ DOES NOT INCLUDE WAR MEDALS.

Index